W.A.S

G000124031

*Grey dawn
breaking*

I must go down to the seas again, to the lonely sea and the sky,
And all I ask is a tall ship and a star to steer her by,
And the wheel's kick and the wind's song and the white sail's shaking,
And a grey mist on the sea's face and a

grey dawn breaking

British merchant seafarers in the late twentieth century

TONY LANE

Manchester University Press

Copyright © A.D. Lane 1986

Published by
Manchester University Press
Oxford Road, Manchester M13 9PL, U.K.
51 Washington Street, Dover, N.H. 03820, U.S.A.

British Library cataloguing in publication data
Lane, Tony
  Grey dawn breaking : British Merchant seafarers
  in the late twentieth century.
  1. Seafaring life — Great Britain   2. Merchant
  seamen — Great Britain
  I. Title
  387.5'4044   VK149

Library of Congress cataloging in publication data
Applied for.

ISBN 0 7190 1876 5 (cased)

CONTENTS

ILLUSTRATIONS

ACKNOWLEDGEMENTS

This book would have been much harder to write without my own experience as a deck apprentice, able seaman and then third and second mate between 1954 and 1963. Just slightly later, while a student in the mid 1960s, I worked in summer vacations for the Merchant Navy and Airline Officers' Association, and this widened my range of contacts and gave me a broad, if indirect, experience beyond my own first-hand knowledge of cargo liners in the Australasian trade and tankers. So all this gave me a good idea of what questions to ask and what exaggerations to discourage when I set off in search of seamen to talk to. To say all this, however, is to glide easily over the sixteen-year gap that had elapsed between my last regular contacts with shipping and seafarers and the research for this book, done in 1983–84. Every year or so in that interim I occasionally met or spoke with my old friend and colleague from the Officers' Association, Bob Elliott, and my debt to him is simply enormous. Rigorously disinterested and scrupulously discreet, Bob has given me many a succinct and painfully accurate briefing on the shipping world.

Another old friend who gave me an excellent briefing was John Prescott. He also helped me to make contacts at the National Union of Seamen, and there I must especially thank Jim Jump and Jack Kinahan at the head office in Clapham and John Mcpherson at the Liverpool branch office. At the head office of the Officers' Association. Claire Walsh, Belinda Pyke and Malcolm Bourne have always been friendly and ready with information.

There have been some complete strangers at the end of telephones who have responded with extraordinary efficiency to small questions of detail that I needed to get right. Among these people Allan Stewart of Denholm's Ship Management sticks in my mind. At the Liverpool Polytechnic Len Holder and Eric Knowles went out of their way to be helpful as well as agreeing to be interviewed. I must also thank Jack Isbester for playing a comparable double role.

There are all those people whose voices fill the following pages, and thank you does not seem enough for all the courtesy, hospitality and good humour. Most of their names appear overleaf, although I must mention here those whom I interviewed but who have not been quoted in the text: Chris King, Phil Emmett, Paul Daunton, Eric Nevin and John Owens all helped me to shape my perspectives, and I owe them quite as much as everyone else I talked to.

The personnel departments of Ocean Fleets, Bibby's, Blue Star and Coe Metcalfe kindly arranged a number of introductions, and I am especially grateful to the management of Sealink, Heysham, for allowing me to spend several days on the *Manx Viking* so that I could interview members of the crew.

Among my colleagues at Liverpool University I am indebted to John Peel and to Colin Henfrey and Joe Melling, who went to a lot of trouble reading and giving good advice on my manuscript. At a more personal level I can only say to Pat Hudson what I have so many times said before: thanks.

There is finally my long-standing debt to Ronald Hope of the Marine Society. There cannot be many seafarers who have tried their hand at writing and who have not gained from his advice and encouragement. I am proud to count myself among his ex-students.

I am grateful to the following people and organisations for providing the photographs used to illustrate the book: R. A. Browne, John Forrest Dagleas, Nick Lane, David Mulholland, Norman Sherry, BP Shipping Ltd, the Marine Society, the Merchant Navy and Airline Officers' Association, and Ocean Transport & Trading PLC. The Society of Authors as the literary representative of the estate of John Masefield kindly agreed to the well known lines from *Sea Fever* appearing on the title page.

A. D. L.

THE SEAFARERS AND OTHERS
QUOTED IN THE TEXT

Matt Bainbridge   a bosun in his fifties; recent experience in gas and chemical carriers.

Howard Benson   a senior radio officer in his forties; now works on ferries on the Irish Sea.

Glen Broughton   a second mate in his twenties; now works on coastal bulkers.

Tom Calder   an engineer in his early sixties; worked on coastal tramps for thirty years.

Peter Carney   a steward in his early thirties; sailed in every type of ship and now in the cross-Channel ferries.

Tony Casson   a bosun in his fifties; worked all his seagoing life for Ocean Fleets.

Ralph Chaplin*   an engineer in his early twenties; works for a tanker company.

John Curry   a Liverpool river pilot in his forties.

John Dooligan   a cook in his early sixties; experience of every type of ship; sailed in the *Queen Elizabeth* during World War II and has recently been to the Falklands.

Bob Evans   padre at the Mersey Mission to Seamen.

Frank Fearon   a steward in his thirties; now works on ferries.

Elizabeth Flynn*   a third mate in her early twenties; worked for a tanker company.

Joe Gallagher   a motorman in his fifties; now works on ferries.

Mick Gibbons   an AB in his early sixties; sunk three times in World War II – twice by U-boat and once by iceberg; now on Irish Sea ferries.

John Goble   a Palm Line mate in his forties; sailed in a number of different trades, recently between Brazil and Australia.

George Hardy*   a master in his early sixties and recently retired from a lifetime's work with Ocean Fleets.

Jack Haywood*   an AB/handyman in his fifties; an ex-joiner who had sailed as carpenter all his adult life; now sails in tankers and bulkers.

Peter Henderson   a cook/chief steward in his thirties; works on Ellerman ships.

Tony Hinks   a petty officer/motorman in his twenties; works for Ocean Fleets.

Mick Hunter   a steward in his thirties; has worked in most of the now defunct passenger ships and is now in ferries.

Peter Hyde   an engineer in his twenties; had been made redundant and was looking for a ship.

Len Holder   ex-mate in Blue Funnel, in his forties; now head of the Department of Maritime Studies, Liverpool Polytechnic.

Jack Isbester   a master in his fifties; worked for Clan Line for many years and now works for Jebsen's.

Janis James   a third mate in her twenties; works for Ocean Fleets.

Mike Johns   a master in his forties; ex-Clan Line and Palm Line, now works for Coe & Metcalfe in coastal tramps.

Tommy Keefe   a cook in his early thirties; various deep-sea trades, now in ferries.

Billy Kerrigan   an ex-bosun in his sixties; recently retired after nearly fifty years at sea.

Jim Kierans   an engine-room storekeeper, just sixty; semi-retired from deep-sea.

Dave Kirkwood*   a general purpose rating in his late thirties; an ex-RN petty officer and recently made redundant from a bulker company.

Eric Knowles   an ex-chief engineer from Blue Funnel and Turnbull Scott, in his fifties; now principal lecturer in marine engineering at Liverpool Polytechnic.

Colum Legatt   a second mate in his late twenties; a graduate in maritime studies and now works for C. Y. Tung.

Dino Livingstone   a motorman in his twenties; worked on the *QE II* and now in ferries.

Hermon McKay*   a motorman in his fifties; a wide experience including working as fireman in a coal-burning ship. now on ships working in and out of the Mersey.

Bernie McNamee   a cook in his early twenties; has worked mainly in ferries.

Andrew Milligan   a mate in his early forties; varied experience and now with Blue Star.

Barney Moussa   an ex-AB in his early sixties; joined his first ship in Dar-es-Salaam in 1943; extensive experience in tramps.

Roger O'Hara   an ex-Blue Funnel engineer in his fifties; has worked ashore for more than twenty years.

Jim O'Kane   a mate in his early forties; now in coastal tramps, where he started as a boy seaman.

Frank Owen*   a master in his early sixties; until recently worked mainly in the Mediterranean trade.

Fred Patten   an ex-master in his sixties; recently retired from Ellerman Papayanni.

Noel Pereira   a second mate in his thirties; an ex-Singapore pilot, recently worked for Worldwide Shipping of Hong Kong.

John Pritchard   a chief engineer in his forties; worked for Bibby's, Harrison's and recently PanOcean.

Barry Roberts   a mate in his twenties; works on North Sea supply boats.

Tony Santamara   a cook in his early forties; wide and varied experience deep-sea, now in ferries.

Jim Slater   General Secretary, National Union of Seamen; ex-bosun.

Anthony Stringfellow   priest, Apostleship of the Sea.

Jack Tanner*   an ex-master in his early sixties; worked mainly in the Mediterranean trades.

Joe Taylor   a cook in his late fifties; varied experience, mainly in passenger ships, now in ferries.

Dario Vieceli   a chief engineer in his early forties; came to the UK in his late 'teens from Italy and sailed on British ships for more than twenty years, now with Ellerman's.

Mike Wake   a third engineer in his twenties; works for Blue Star.

Chris Warlow   a third mate with Shell, in his early twenties.

Emlyn Williams   an AB in his late twenties; on the Pool and takes what ships he can.

Frank Williams   a second cook in his twenties; varied experience, now in ferries.

Rodney Wilson   an ex-cook/chief steward in his early sixties; retired early and reluctantly from Ellerman's.

Jack Woods   a master in his forties; unusually varied experience in tramps, cargo liners, tankers, now in ferries.

* Pseudonym.

That crew of Liverpool hard cases had in them the right stuff. It's my experience they always have. It is the sea that gives it … – *Joseph Conrad*

[I] · *Introduction*

a good look.
you might not
e chance.

The Liner she's a lady, an' she never looks nor 'eeds –
The Man-o'-War's 'er 'usband, an' 'e gives 'er all she needs;
But, oh, the little cargo-boats, that sail the wet seas roun',
They're just the same as you an' me a-plyin' up an' down!

The Liner she's a lady by the paint upon 'er face,
An' if she meets an accident they count it sore disgrace:
The Man-o'-War's 'er 'usband, and 'e's always 'andy by,
But, oh, the little cargo-boats! they've got to load or die.

The Liner she's a lady, and 'er route is cut an' dried;
The Man-o'-War's 'er 'usband, an' 'e always keeps beside;
But, oh, the little cargo-boats that 'aven't any man,
They've got to do their business first, and make the most they can!

The Liner she's a lady, and if a war should come,
The Man-o'-War's 'er 'usband, and 'e'd bid 'er stay at home;
But, oh, the little cargo-boats that fill with every tide!
'E'd 'ave to up an' fight for them, for they are England's pride.

The Liner she's a lady, but if she wasn't made,
There still would be the cargo-boats for 'ome an' foreign trade.
The Man-o'-War's 'er 'usband, but if we wasn't 'ere,
'E wouldn't have to fight at all for 'ome an' friends so dear.

Rudyard Kipling

Considering how many of Britain's traditional industries have simultaneously shrunk and been turned inside out over the last decade, it is remarkable to find how little of any of this has been recorded. Of course the changes have been logged in memories and passed on in piecemeal conversational snatches, but knowledge of this sort is half private, almost the privileged information of families and occupational communities. Perhaps it is because so little knowledge of what has changed has passed into popular currency, beyond the fact of change itself, that so many people are plainly puzzled and disoriented.

Part of the difficulty of understanding the nature of industrial change and its social consequences is that people like seafarers, along with shipbuilders, steelmakers, foundrymen, machine-tool builders, are all 'minorities'. But taken together they account for a very large piece indeed of British experience of present times. Ought we not then to assume that through them we may learn a great deal about our collective experience of what is plainly a critical period?

This book attempts to capture the changes and continuities of the seafaring life; to show how seafarers construct and inherit a particular image of themselves, to portray the social relations of a cramped and hierarchical community, to describe accurately and explain the significance of the daily routines of shipboard life and the nature of hazards and voyages. It is always hard to know how to make a convincing leap of generalisation from the particular experiences of one group of people, and this seems especially true of seafarers, whose isolation would seem to guarantee them a high degree of uniqueness. And yet, for all of that, for all the fact that a ship is neither an office nor a factory, there are many underlying aspects of the seafarer's life that connect with the daily experience of being British in the closing decades of the twentieth century. Among the more familiar themes which weave the lives of seafarers into those of others are the pervasive inequalities and prejudices of class, the opaque and tortuous legacy of empire, the chasm between those who own and control industry and those who are expected to work unquestioningly in it. These are the familiar structural questions of social science; the questions of class, status, ideology and power and the specific forms they take in a particular period of history.

While this study is patently informed by and concerned with these issues, only occasionally have they been allowed into the foreground and at no point have they been given extended treatment in theoretical discussion. The resort to a narrative method built out of direct speech has ensured only a lurking presence for the 'big questions' asked by social scientists, although the muting of these questions has also been a matter of deliberate choice.

Even though this book centres on the condition of contemporary seafarers, the essential time frame is the period from the mid-1950s onward. There are points at which it has been necessary to listen to experiences from the 1930s and the Second World War. Sometimes, fragments of historical analysis reaching back into the later nineteenth century have been inserted into the narrative when understanding of a question would be impaired without it. Only in this introductory chapter is there any chronological account of developments in the shipping industry. A working knowledge of these matters is absolutely essential, for it is these which have so profoundly transformed the life of the British seafarer.

It is a simple and observable matter of fact that in their every-day lives people do not as a rule think of themselves as historical actors, pushed and propelled by structural forces which are beyond their individual reach and control. The actual day-to-day business of living is what presses hardest. In this study, therefore, I have tried to capture the everyday life of seafaring and to allow the big questions only to intrude and take as much space as they do 'naturally'. In terms of the broad spread of what is now conventional social scientific practice this technique might seem a little odd and perhaps rather old-fashioned: the most obvious genre comparisons are with Mark Benney's mining study, *Charity Main*, first published in 1946, and with Ferdynand Zweig's general books on working-class life, *Labour, Life and Poverty* and *The British Worker*, published in 1949 and 1952 respectively.

Considering the emphasis in patriotic rhetoric on Britain's 'maritime greatness' it is remarkable how little has been written about merchant seafarers. There is some irony in noticing that among the first words of the last comprehensive account of merchant seamen, its author, Frank Bullen, said, 'Go where you will, up and down this country of ours, and, except among people directly engaged in shipping business, or a few earnest souls ..., you will find scarcely any knowledge of the British Merchant Service at all.'[1] The book was published in 1900.

There is a sparse social science literature on seafarers, but almost all of it has been written from within the framework of social engineering and accordingly focuses on what are seen as the 'problems' of being a seafarer. An excellent representation of this is to be found in the collection of essays edited by Peter Fricke, *Seafarer and Community*.[2] Without exception the essays are concerned with 'problems of adaptation' to the community of ship and shore. The most recent contributions by social scientists, contained in Robert Schrank's *Industrial Democracy at Sea*,[3] are also firmly in the social engineering tradition.

Far more interesting, as a rule, is the extensive and regularly replenished memoir literature. Although mainly written by ship-masters, it is nevertheless a very useful source for the social historian, and I have found it invaluable in identifying the nuances of the manners and morals of deck officers.[4] Far more wide-ranging in their content and in the ranks of their authors are three anthologies of essays and short stories written by merchant seamen about merchant seamen. The contributions were all originally harvested by the Seafarers' Education Service (now the Marine Society), cover the period from the 1930s and must be absolutely unique in the sense that no other industry could muster anything remotely comparable.[5]

Running parallel to the anthologised seafarers is the continuing tradition of novel-writing by ex-merchant seafarers (a number of whom started on their literary careers with the Seafarers' Education Service). The range of work in this form is large, varied, extremely uneven and always interesting. At the lighter end are Humfrey Jordan's popular and romantic novels, mainly written in the 1930s, providing an interesting if unintended commentary on the social aspirations of passenger ship officers.[6] Written in the same period but far weightier and as close to the bone of seafaring as any writer has ever got (Conrad not excluded) are James Hanley's early novels.[7] Malcolm Lowry's *Ultramarine* has, of course, gone through a number of printings in the last twenty years. Although Lowry made only one voyage to sea when in his late 'teens, he nevertheless ranks alongside Hanley in his skilful probing of the existential bleaknesses of the seafaring life that have only fleetingly been touched upon in this study. Conscious of their social isolation and sensitive to its personal consequences, seamen are adept at maintaining a public front of stoicism. The same seems to apply even when seamen write poetry. In a really excellent collection of verse assembled by the Marine Society[8] there is realism and romance but very little *angst*.

All except two of the interviews were tape-recorded. Most people received transcripts of their interviews, and in these cases I have used only passages approved by the informant. Some people have wanted to remain completely anonymous, while others have agreed that I might sometimes quote them by name. A few people never returned amended transcripts, and a handful of interviews were snatched in public places. Because of these variations the names which appear in the text are a mixture of real ones and pseudonyms. I have used real names only where I have had explicit permission to do so.

In total, I spoke with sixty-five men and two women and so

far as possible tried to assemble a pool of people who had gone to sea at different times between the mid-1930s and the mid-1980s. I was also concerned to ensure that I talked to people of different ranks from the deck, engine-room and catering departments. Having no research funding of any kind whatsoever, I was obliged to interview people living on Merseyside and elsewhere in the North West and North Wales. I do not think this has in any way affected the material except sometimes in the colour and vigour of expression.

In every interview I looked for much the same type of information, and the chapter headings are a faithful representation of the type of questions I asked and the answers I got. Apart from three people who have professionally associated with seafarers for many years, everyone interviewed has had extensive sea experience. Several gave up the sea a number of years ago but have been in jobs dependent upon everyday contact with ships and their crews.

I found people to talk with wherever I could – some in the offices of the various trade unions, others in the International Seafarers' Centre on the Liverpool waterfront. I was also introduced to people through the personnel offices of shipowners and friendly colleagues at the Liverpool Polytechnic. Apart from the fact that I knew I had to speak to people of different age and rank I knew, too, that I had to find some women seafarers. There have been women seafarers since the nineteenth century, when they sailed on passenger ships as nurses and stewardesses. Much more recently there have been women navigators, radio officers, pursers and handfuls of engineers. The first women officer cadets were recruited in the mid-1960s, and I have been told that the first woman to go to sea in that rank is now a chief officer. She has about fifty other female officer colleagues. Too late for this book I heard about a female owner-master of a coaster whom I would definitely have sought out.

I

Just thirty years ago, in 1955, shipping was bathing in the post-war boom, and shipowners queued at the yards of the Clyde and the Tyne for new tonnage. The world's ports were full of red ensigns. Imperial dependencies upon which the industry had grown and prospered were still strong. The British people were pleased to be able to convince themselves that they still had an empire by calling it a Commonwealth, and self-delusion was particularly easy for seamen. It might be that Britain's merchant ships did not as decisively dominate world trade as they had in the Edwardian years but this was still, and by a large margin, the biggest fleet at sea and trading.

Ten years later, in 1965, it was still possible in the seaports to see, smell and hear the evidence of a great trading nation with a satellite Empire-Commonwealth. The Bank Line brought in copra from the South Pacific islands, Elder Dempster's palm kernels and groundnuts from Nigeria, Blue Funnel discharged hardwoods and latex from Borneo and Malaya, Shaw Savill carried wool from Australia and the Port Line frozen lamb from New Zealand. Every corner of the Empire-Commonwealth and many another notionally independent country was tied by trade to the UK and linked to a British quayside by fleets of ships owned in Liverpool, London, Glasgow, Hull, the Tyne and ports of the Bristol Channel. But within all this activity was decline.

Throughout the post-war years the number of British ships and the number of seamen have consistently fallen. In 1950 there were over 3,300 ships but by the end of 1984 only 940 or so. This huge reduction in fleet size embraces a number of other changes which have transformed the seafaring life. The decline of empire, the expansion of trade with Europe, changes in types of ship, in voyage patterns, company ownership, size of crew and division of labour, the nature of work and the social environment of the ship have combined to turn the seagoing life upside down.

Change began slowly enough in the late 1950s and gathered pace in the late 1960s as the first container ships appeared, and again in the early 1970s as the expanding petrochemical industry called for more and more gas and chemical carriers. And yet by 1985 there was little left of what there had been before, and the British merchant fleet was beginning to look as if it would soon consist only of cross-Channel ferries and the elongated tugs serving the platforms and rigs of the North Sea and Morecambe Bay. But in 1975 there was enough left of traditional shipping and trade routes for young people, starting a seagoing life in their mid-'teens, to feel part of long-standing ways of thinking and doing things. It is only in the last ten years that the changes have become complete, and so most seafarers over the age of twenty-eight have vivid recollections of a way of life that, although now gone for ever, will be constantly there to unsettle the present. Without the embroidery of memory they will be able to say truthfully that yesterday was better.

By the turn of the century shipowners in the UK had almost completely given up on sailing ships in foreign trade, and so dominant had British steam shipping become that it carried half the world's trade and virtually all the trade to and from the countries of Empire. Liverpool and London had the world's most extensive dock systems and both were liner ports. If the passenger ships of such companies as the Cunard and the P & O seemed to preside over these places by virtue of their size and grandeur, most liners were actually cargo ships that might or might not carry passengers and whose real business was running scheduled services to and from nominated destinations.

Well before the turn of the century all world regions with an external trade were served by regular sailings from Liverpool and London. If there was no direct route to a port that a shipper wanted to reach, there was always the possibility that crates and bales could be off-loaded into a smaller ship and sent to a trading post, manned by an expatriate, and too small and remote to be noticed in the household atlas.

On the coasts of West Africa, Peru and Chile, India, Ceylon, Burma, the Persian Gulf, in the island chains of the Caribbean and in the rivers and archipelagos of South East Asia and the South Pacific there were fleets of ships with British officers and local crews. These were ships that rarely, if ever, went back to the UK once they had left the builder's yard. Small and handy, with shallow draughts many of them, they went up the creeks and rivers and took cargoes in small parcels off remote beaches and islands for delivery to the larger ports served by the liners. The officers who sailed on these ships were waterborne residents of the regions they traded in and might go home only at five-year intervals. Many of these feeder services survived the Second World War, and Straits Steam, based in Singapore, was only sold off by Ocean Transport, its UK parent, in 1983.[9]

Celebrated more in the verse of Rudyard Kipling than in the hearts of seamen were the tramps of the Tyne and the Bristol

Channel which distributed steam coal to the coaling stations of the world's shipping routes. Port Said, Perim, Las Palmas, Cape Town were their destinations – and thereafter anywhere according to season to find a cargo. It might be case oil from Baku in the Black Sea to Colombo or grain from New Orleans to Antwerp. Tramps and their crews would never know where they were going next or when they would be home.

After the First World War the British merchant fleet formed a steadily falling proportion of world shipping, although at the outbreak of the Second World War it was still the world's largest fleet and remained so in the post-war period into the 1960s. The liner networks in particular were still there in the 1960s; their remnants traded into the 1970s until succeeded by their modern counterparts, the container ships.

In terms of where they took the ships, what they carried and how long they were away, the men who sailed on the cargo liners into the 1970s were doing much the same as their predecessors had been doing before the First World War. The twin-engined motor ship *Hinakura*, owned by the P & O subsidiary The New Zealand Shipping Company, was a typical Clyde-built refrigerated cargo liner on the Australia/New Zealand run from 1950 to 1974. On a normal five-month round voyage she would have sailed from Liverpool, London or Avonmouth and arrived five weeks later at the first Australian port, say Fremantle. A month later she would be discharging the last of her outward cargo at Brisbane, having called at Adelaide, Melbourne and Sydney. She might then go up to some of the Barrier Reef ports like Townsville and Bowen to load meat, wool, sugar, rice, canned fruit. After perhaps no more than a few days in each port it would then be back down to Brisbane, Sydney, Melbourne, Adelaide to take in big consignments of meat, top off with a tarpaulin-covered deck cargo of bales of wool – and then another five-week trip home through the Suez Canal, with an intermediate stop at Aden for bunkers.[10]

Today this run is covered by container ships the size of the *Queen Elizabeth II* (known as Panamax ships because they are the maximum size compatible with the locks and bends in the Panama Canal) that can lift the cargoes of six *Hinakura*s in one load, do the round voyage in half the time, run at a speed increased by 50 per cent and carry crews reduced by more than half.

Similar changes have affected the liner trades across the Atlantic to Canada, the east and west coasts of the USA and the Caribbean. Container ships also monopolise the liner trades to the Mediterranean and the Far East. Only in the African and Latin American trades are conventional ships still to be found, though very few are now British.

Just as the trading patterns of the cargo liners of the 1950s and 1960s were little changed in fifty years, much the same was true of the tramps. The life of an early 1960s tramp was no less erratic than those of the 1890s. Frequently hired to carry just one cargo between two ports, neither of them in northern Europe, to be away from home for two years at a stretch was by no means unusual.

An excellent example is the Cardiff-owned *Redbrook*, which sailed from Bremerhaven for Alexandria with a cargo of coke in March 1962 and arrived back in Leith twenty-seven months later, in May 1964. In the interim the *Redbrook* carried cement from Odessa to India, rice from Rangoon to Ceylon, coal from Calcutta to Bombay, iron ore from Bombay to Rumania, cotton from Port Sudan to Spain and Italy, grain from Turkey to Japan, logs from Borneo to Italy, chrome ore from Casablanca to Japan, timber and general cargo from Vancouver and San Francisco to the Fiji islands and New Zealand and finally a full cargo of barley from Western Australia to Leith.[11]

Today's tramps are more likely to be called dry bulk carriers and they are much bigger and more specialised than the *Redbrooks* were. But they live similar lives. Sometimes it might be a charter to carry so many cargoes within a given time period between nominated ports, at another time the hire might be for just one cargo. The flavour of the life of these ships is perfectly caught in the no-words-wasted prose of the daily report on the dry cargo markets on the backpage of *Lloyds List*. The following is an extract from a report from the Baltic Exchange early in February 1985:

... a Swiss-flag vessel under time charter to an Italian company was said to have been fixed for 52,000 tons of heavy grain, sorghum and soya beans ... while charterers were thought to have found cover for between 3,000 and 5,000 tons of barley on an unnamed vessel from the North Pacific to Mina Jebel Ali [in the Persian Gulf].[12]

Voyage patterns in tankers might differ very little from those in tramps. While the oil companies like Shell, BP and Esso usually had the largest tanker fleets, they never built anything like enough tonnage to cover their world-wide requirements and therefore chartered ships from independent owners. Although from the late 1950s the liner companies scented a boom market and began to build tanker tonnage and then hire it out on long-term charters to the oil companies, a large proportion of British-flag independent tankers were owned by the tramp companies.

The oil companies ran some of their ships almost as liners – virtually all of Esso's deep-sea fleet ran regularly between Fawley or Milford Haven and Middle East ports. Shell and BP, on the other hand, were notorious for their long and uncertain voyages. With refineries in such places as Iran, Aden, Indonesia and Australia, crews on these ships could quite easily find that once they had left a European port they were running thereafter from the Persian Gulf to practically anywhere bordering the Indian Ocean or the South Pacific.[13] The same uncertainties still apply to tankers and to the newer gas carriers.

The passenger liners were in a wholly different world. Subsidised by mail contracts, these were the ships that linked the islands and land masses of empire and got noticed in *The Times* when delayed by fog in the English Channel.[14] They were not every seafarer's taste and were often disparagingly called 'cattle boats'. Air travel killed off this branch of the industry. Nevertheless, over 600,000 people arrived and departed at UK ports from non-European countries in 1959, and until well into the 1960s it remained possible to travel in some style to India and the Far East, Australasia, the USA and Canada, to the Caribbean and Latin America, to Africa south, east and west. Excluding the current summer passages by the *QE II* from Southampton to New York, the last scheduled passenger ship sailing was as late as 1977, when the *Windsor Castle* sailed for Cape Town. Successors to these ships are the cruise liners. Based semi-permanently in the Caribbean and other brochured regions of island fantasy, they are self-propelled up-market Benidorms.

The old passenger ships invariably ran to tight schedules and in this sense, if in no other, were twins to the ferries that linked Britain to Ireland and the Continent. Before the large-scale development of car-borne tourism most ferries were run by

British Rail, which had of course inherited them from the railway companies. The ferries were run in the practices of the railways: they had graded and uniformed staff who were drilled in a strict adherence and respect for the timetable. Despite these disciplines the jobs were, and remain, sought after. With their short trips they were the next best thing to a home-every-night job.

Coastal confreres to the ferry men are those who run the small – but sometimes very large – ships around the UK coast, into the Baltic and to ports anywhere between northern Norway and Oporto.[15] Just within the UK some 40 per cent of domestic freight is carried by ship, and the growth of trade between Britain and Europe has greatly increased short-sea trading. Apart from the container and the RO-RO ships, which are mainly owned by the ferry companies, coastal cargoes are usually bulk something or other. The dry bulk commodities such as coal, grain and animal feeds are carried interchangeably on the same ships. Oil, gas and chemicals are each carried in specialist ships, and some of the oil tankers using North Sea terminals are very large.

II

The names of shipping companies quoted on the stock exchange in the 1960s accounted for only a small proportion of the names of shipowners familiar to seafarers. Family ownership in private firms was still common, and some of them were among the largest in Europe. The best known of them was Ellerman's, with a fleet of about ninety ships, owned by the founder's millionaire son, who was a recluse with an obsessive interest in rats. Ellerman ships were active in trades to the Baltic, Portugal and the Mediterranean, South Africa, India and Australia. The next largest family firm was owned by the Vesteys, who besides the Dewhurst chain of shops and Union Cold Storage owned the Blue Star Line, running to the east coast of South America and Australasia, the Booth Line running via Portugal and the Caribbean and Brazil, and Lamport & Holt's, which served Brazil and Argentina.

Other sizeable family-owned fleets were T. & J. Harrison's in the trades to the Caribbean and Mexican Gulf and South and East Africa, Andrew Weir's Bank Line, trading to the South Pacific islands and the Far East, the Thomson family's Ben Line, which ran just about the smartest and fastest British cargo liners to China and Japan, and then Bibby's, with ships going to India, Ceylon and Burma.

Family ownership was just as common in the tramp and independent tanker trades. The *Redbrook*, for example, was owned by one man, and there were many other small fleets of perhaps one to five ships wholly in family ownership. The same applied in the coastal trades, although owner-captains, common in the Dutch and West German coastal fleets, mostly disappeared when the last of the sailing barges and schooners went out of the estuarial and coastal trades.[16]

Despite the fact that most of the large tramp and liner fleets were wholly owned subsidiaries of the public companies whose shares were traded on the stock exchange, family influence and even control were pervasive. The largest group, P&O, had more or less completed its acquisitions by the end of the First World War – but in many of the subsidiary companies family shareholdings had frequently been large enough to allow the families to retain control. Much the same pattern applied in Cunard and in the Furness Withy group. The two other large public liner companies, British & Commonwealth and Ocean Steam, had many fewer subsidiaries and in all but name and legal status were family firms. The larger tramp companies such as Jacob's, Common Bros, Ropner's and Reardon Smith's were also public companies under family control.

Coast Lines and General Steam were the largest liner operators in the coastal and near Continental trades, and although both were P&O subsidiaries there were strong family interests in each of them. It was only the tanker fleets, owned by the oil majors, which were run by professional managers who did not owe their position to family shareholdings.

If major changes were forced upon shipowners by international developments from the 1960s onward, families continue to play an important, though reduced, role in this most secretive of industries. Until the 1960s the shipping world was as closed and elitist as banking and finance. The tight little shipowning communities centred around Water Street in Liverpool and Leadenhall Street and St Mary Axe in London maintained family control by avoiding bank loans and issues of new share capital. However, the advent of containerisation and growing competition from owners flying different national flags demanded drastic survival strategies. Draconian reorganisation of internal management was forced upon the subsidiaries of Cunard, Furness Withy and P&O, and the huge costs of containerisation drove the big public companies and the larger family liner firms into new consortia run by a new breed of professional managers.[17]

The biggest of the British container consortia, Overseas Containers Ltd (OCL), is principally owned by P&O, Ocean Transport and British & Commonwealth. Its fleet consists of nine Panamax ships running to the Far East and Australasia. Cunard are involved in two separate consortia: with Dutch, Swedish and West German firms in Atlantic Containers Ltd (ACL) on the North Atlantic service, and with Blue Star and Ellerman's in Associated Container Transport (ACT), with a service to Australasia via South Africa.

In that extraordinarily hectic period for the shipping industry, the mid-'60s to the mid-'70s, it was not only containerisation and company reorganisation that promoted change. The mighty Cunard got absorbed into the Trafalgar House group, to sit alongside hotels, construction firms and property developers, while P&O took over firms engaged in similar areas as well as in road haulage. As the 1970s progressed more and more shipping firms diversified: Ellerman's into travel promotion and brewing, British & Commonwealth into financial services and biotechnology, Ocean into warehousing and other activities adjacent to shipping. The quoted tramp and tanker companies made comparable moves, and many of the big names in shipping, including P&O, set up subsidiaries to supply and service the new offshore oil and gas producing industry.

It was during these years, 1965 to 1975, that there were far-reaching changes in the types of ship available for seafarers to work aboard. The passenger ships finally went altogether, under the impact of airline competition. Next to go were the traditional cargo liners. The trades to the more advanced industrial and trading countries were quickly taken over by container ships. In the second rank of world trading nations, in such countries as India, Chile, Nigeria, governments were anxious to save on foreign currencies and encouraged the development of national fleets. Now displaced from these markets, many of the traditional cargo liner companies began to move into the bulk trades.

Financially this was a good time to be thinking of building new tonnage, for the Wilson government of 1966–70 and the Heath government of 1970–74 were both heavily subsidising new building in UK shipyards. It was in this period that the Bibby family, for example, switched from owning cargo liners to bulk carriers and in the process expanded their fleet to a size bigger than at any other time in the past.[18]

This, of course, was the time when tankers and dry bulkers were getting bigger and bigger and the terminology was going up-scale, from Very Large Crude Carrier (VLCC) to Ultra Large Crude Carrier (ULCC).[19] It was also the period when gasfields were being increasingly exploited and when there seemed no limit to the growth in demand for the special chemicals and gases used by the plastic, fertiliser and artificial fibre industries. Here once again consortia were being created (one including Ocean and P&O) to build gas and chemical carriers, although family firms like Bibby and Turnbull Scott built specialist tonnage to their own account.

By the mid-1980s almost all the traditional ship types, of which there had still been an abundance in 1975, had gone, except in the coastal trades. And yet ownership of ships continued in some aspects to have a familiar look. It was true that Ellerman's had been sold by the family trust into public ownership in 1983, that Harrison's were down to one ship in their own colours, that British & Commonwealth looked like any other conglomerate and that Trafalgar House, having failed to take over P&O, was whispering that it would like to sell Cunard to P & O. But, for all that, the Vestey family still owned a large fleet, and family-owned and family-controlled firms were still common. In 1985 the family-controlled forty-strong Everard fleet of coasters and short-sea traders, once the butt of jokes and lordly disdain from deep-sea liner men, was one of the few dynamic shipping firms, and jobs in its ships were sought after by men from the shrinking deep-sea fleets.

In the background of all the developments that have transformed the shipping industry have been powerful international influences. These are signified in the Bahamian flag worn by several Cunard cruise ships, the thirty-five UK-owned ships registered in Monrovia and the 120 registered in Panama. The resort by British shipowners to the Liberian and Panamanian flags on this scale is fairly recent, although resort to flags of convenience by UK owners is far from new: in the early 1960s several of P&O's new tankers were registered in Bermuda.

Flags of convenience were first adopted by US shipowners in the 1920s, and the motives then were the same as they were subsequently in the post-war years when the Liberian and Panamian fleets grew rapidly.[20] After the First World War US owners were looking for ways to escape US crew wage rates, and they were doing the same after 1945. American shipowners continue to own the largest flag-of-convenience fleets, although in more recent years Greek, Hong Kong Chinese and Japanese owners have also adopted the registries of Liberia and Panama on a large scale. A recurring reason is the avoidance of national flag wage rates, though there are other advantages such as tax avoidance and escape from creditors.[21]

From the 1960s onwards, British crew costs were falling relative to those in the other European and Japanese fleets and taxation was easy to avoid in the UK. In these circumstances there were no great incentives to British owners to 'flag out'. However, by the early 1980s freight rates had fallen so far that everywhere in world shipping there was a rush to cut crew costs. It was for exactly these reasons that Bibby's transferred their ships to the Bermudan flag, sacked their remaining British ratings and replaced them with Chinese.[22]

All British seafarers have been affected by the international search by shipowners for ever cheaper sources of seagoing labour. Only a relative and temporary shortage of experienced officers in the middle range has given British officers more shelter than British ratings. As for the shipowners themselves, it is clear that for many of them deep-sea operations will continue to be a dwindling activity. Shortly before his death in 1982 C.Y. Tung said that the centre of gravity of world shipping had now moved to South East Asia and the Far East. This seems irrefutable now that the world's second largest merchant fleet appears to be Hong Kong-owned and the largest is Japanese.

III

Liverpool seafarers were understandably angry when they learned that Bibby's had decided to 'flag out' and sack their British ratings. The anger, though, was not so much at the prospect of ships with Chinese crews as with the fact that henceforward *all* Bibby ships would have foreign ratings.

Bibby's, of course, along with every other British shipowner trading to India, Ceylon and Burma, had manned some of their ships with the sons of empire since the late nineteenth century and had never stopped doing so. While all Bibby ships have had British officers, out of a fleet of nine ships in 1982 five had British ratings, two had Chinese and another two had Indians. By 1983 the two ships with Indian crews had been sold but the two others with Chinese remained.

There has never been a time in modern history when large numbers of foreign and Commonwealth seamen have not been employed on British ships. Scandinavians, Germans, French and Italians were frequently employed on sailing ships in the second half of the nineteenth century, while Indians have been periodically employed since the seventeenth century. By the end of the eighteenth century Indians – by then known as Lascars – were employed in large numbers on the ships of the East India Company. A campaign against their employment on ships trading to the UK led to their removal early in the nineteenth century, but by mid-century they were once again in regular employment, this time on the ships of the P&O. From that time forward their numbers employed in ships trading to India and elsewhere steadily increased. By the end of the First World War substantial numbers of Chinese, West Africans, Yemenis, Adenese, Somalis and Zanzibaris were also being employed. The proportion of ratings on British ships from all these areas continued to increase, and by the early 1970s made up 37 per cent of all ratings.

The normal pattern was for shipowners to recruit crews from the countries their ships regularly visited: P&O and Ellerman's from the Indian subcontinent; Elder Dempster's from West Africa; Blue Funnel and Ben Line from China, Hong Kong and Singapore; Harrison's from Barbados. There were also a number of tramp companies with crews from Commonwealth-Empire countries, and they often recruited Arabic people from the Sudan, Somalia, Aden, the Yemen and Zanzibar. It was through the engagement of such crews and the later settlement of some of them in the UK that Cardiff, 'Shields and Liverpool acquired what are usually (and erroneously) called 'Somali' communities.

For its passenger ships the P&O recruited different sections of the crew from different cultural regions of India. The deck crews from the fishing and seafaring villages near Bombay were Hindu; the engine-room crews from the Punjab and the North West Frontier were Islamic; the catering crews came from Christian Goa. Apart from the officers, the only other white crew members were the quartermasters (helmsmen) and they, in accordance with the 'rules' of imperial management, had petty officer status although in a ship with a European crew they would have been classed as ratings.

Ratings in the various shipboard departments have often been drawn from different ethnic origins. In some Blue Funnel ships the catering and engine-room ratings were Chinese while the deck crowd was British. In the Palm Line the catering department was Nigerian, the engine-room ratings UK-domiciled 'Somali' and the deck crowd British. Only in tramps were departments themselves ethnically mixed, but even there it was normal for the engine-room ratings to be ethnically of the one origin.

Although there has been at least one UK ship with a black captain and there have been handfuls of Indian, Sri Lankan and Chinese officers, ethnic variation has been common only among ratings. From the 1950s onward, cadets from ex-imperial countries were sometimes trained on British ships for deck officer status, but apart from the stewards waiting at table they were the only people likely to be found in a ship's saloon who were not white and British.

Over the last ten years the numbers of Asian and African seamen on British ships have dwindled. The steadily increasing pressure of unemployment has led the National Union of Seamen to adopt the policy of British-level wages being paid on all British ships. The progressive application of this policy has tended to eliminate wage competition between British and say Indian or Bangla Deshi and the shipowner has found a shrinking advantage in employing non-British crews. On the other hand, and as we have already seen, the unrelenting recession has seen owners revert to Third World crews by the simple expedient of 'flagging out'.

Crew size used to vary with ethnic origin, and until quite recent years the difference in wage rates still made it economic for a shipowner to take an Indian crew that was much larger than one hired in Europe. Indeed, where Indian and Bangla Deshi seafarers were concerned the rule of thumb in the 1960s was much the same as it had been at the turn of the century: two Indians for every one European. By the 1980s, however, the ratio had changed to three Indian to two European.

Matters of ethnic origin aside, crew size varied more with the type of trade a ship was in than its size. Passenger ships naturally had the largest crews. The *Queens* had crews in excess of 1,000 and the present *QE II* has a crew of about 800. Even the smaller ships sailing to New Zealand had crews that ran into the hundreds. With an elaborate pecking order and the petty corruptions of a big hotel, these ships had none of the simplicity of the social division of labour on the cargo liner, tramp and tanker. The passenger ships tended to attract the hustlers and those officers with a taste for a uniformed regime and a quasi-naval hierarchy.

Elsewhere the cargo liners usually had bigger crews than the tramps, and this was due to the fact that they had more sophisticated engine rooms and more cargo-handling gear to maintain. The cargo liners also operated under the shelter of stable cartels, and this allowed their owners to indulge their officers by adding to their number and themselves by providing enough ABs to maintain a yacht-like appearance to their ships. The officers on this type of ship, especially those on the Australasian run, thought of themselves as something of an elite and like their passenger ship colleagues believed in wearing their uniform with a naval respect for correct detail. Some of these companies also kept their own 'pools' of ratings from particular regions: the Port Line preferred Shetlanders and the New Zealand Shipping Company Hebrideans.

Tramps operated in a more uncertain environment and were usually much more bareboned: they were less technically sophisticated, spent less on cosmetics and maintenance and had smaller crews. Tramp deck officers were much more likely to have worked their way up from AB, and, while they were as jealous as any liner officer of the ship's appearance, cared little for the observances of uniform. Where manning scales are concerned the *Redbrook* again provides a useful example. In 1963 she had a total crew of thirty-six, which compared with a complement of forty-eight when she was run as a refrigerated cargo liner by Blue Star.

The large tankers of the early 1960s had crews of about forty-five men regardless of whether it was a 20,000 tonner or a 100,000 tonner. The ships of Shell and BP were run with much the same punctilious attention to detail and formality as the cargo liners, although conditions of service were much superior on the Esso ships, where tramp attitudes prevailed.

Where the coastal ferries had manning levels and hierarchical observances which were on a par with the deep-sea cargo liners, the run-of-the-mill coaster would have a crew of about a dozen and mates and engineers who had begun in the ships as boys. Men would stay in these ships until they went to the breakers' yards, and it would be a normal sequence to start as a boy and end as skipper without ever having entered a classroom in the interim.

There are still many old-time coasting men about but they are a dying breed as new regulations require the next generation of mates, skippers and engineers to have certificates of competency appropriate to the trades their ships are in. The coaster's crew, just like that of all other types of ship, has also been steadily reduced. On the most modern coastal bulkers there may be only a six-man crew.

The tramps, cargo liners and tankers being built as late as 1965 were the last of a line. Containerisation, new ship types to carry the traditional bulk cargoes of coal, grain, ore and oil and specialist ships to meet the demand of the petrochemical industry came with a stream of labour-saving innovations to simultaneously impose huge reductions in crew size, shade certain areas of the division of labour and transform voyage patterns everywhere to equivalence with tankers.[23]

Containerisation cleared the decks of all cargo-handling gear and thus reduced the cargo liner's deck crowd from fifteen men to about six. Automation in the engine room has led to a reduction in the total of officers and ratings from about fifteen to seven. Catering staffs have also been cut, from about ten down to six or seven. These figures only give an indication of order of magnitude. The precise manning levels and division of labour always varied with company practice, and the number of crew required operationally has invariably exceeded the minimum laid down by statute, for safety reasons. In the catering department only one qualified cook is required by regulations. It is the hallmarks of status that call for the carriage of stewards so that officers might be waited upon at table and have their accommodation cleaned.

The numbers of seamen employed in the shipping industry are not determined solely by the size of a crew. Leave requirements mean that every ship has more than one crew. With a normal tour of duty of between four and a half and five months, each deep-sea ship has 1·8 crews, which allows leave of roughly one month ashore for two spent at sea. On the ferries, where crews work more intensively, the number of seafarers per ship is much increased, although these vary with the number of sailings. On the Sealink ferries from Dover there are 4·8 crews per ship but 2·5 crews on the Irish ferries from Holyhead. None of this, of course, remotely compares with the much more strictly regulated airlines, where on the long-haul routes there are nine crews per plane.

The division of labour on the ferries between deck, engineering and catering departments is rigid. On deep-sea ships there is more flexibility, though overlapping is confined almost entirely to ratings. On an ocean-going container ship with a crew of perhaps twenty the stewards might turn out to help the ABs when tying up alongside a wharf, and at sea some ABs might help out with a heavy job in the engine room. Among the officers there is a tendency for the radio officer's role to be extended into the maintenance of electronic equipment. But the engineers have nothing to do with navigation or the loading and discharge of cargo, the mates have nothing to do with the main engines and auxiliaries, and neither have anything to do with catering except to complain at its product.

The mates and engineers have identical hierarchies of rank, wear equivalent amounts of gold braid and are paid much the same salaries – but the chain of command is through the deck department. The chief engineer may have four stripes on his sleeve in the same way as the captain but the ship's second-in-command is the chief officer (the mate).

Talk of 'tours of duty' in the manner of the armed forces and of the old corps of imperial administrators is a clear illustration that the length of a stay aboard ship is no longer a function of the length of a voyage, which begins and ends in a UK or near Continental port. The only scheduled services with a UK terminus are the container ships, and these employ a minority of a deep-sea men and women. Cruise ships, bulkers and the different types of tanker do most of their voyages between foreign ports. A crew change is far more likely in New York or New Orleans than in Liverpool or London.

Once aboard for a tour of duty, the deck officers and ratings who keep the sea watch cycle of four hours on and eight hours off are unlikely to break this routine unless the ship has a port stay of more than thirty-six hours. This possibility is increasingly rare, for only on the disappearing general cargo ships are turn-around times measured in days. Even a coaster with a bulk cargo can expect to enter a port on one tide and leave it on the next, twelve hours later. For the seafarer of today it is a bonus to enter a port where the only bulk handling gear is a five-ton crane with a grab; or for a tanker or gas carrier to find that it is pumping into a narrow-gauge pipeline and into storage tanks that are uphill and a mile away. Ports with these qualities, provided there is a town near by, have become the stuff of anticipatory gossip in saloon and messroom.

Employment in the shipping industry for ABs, stewards and greasers was quite unlike work anywhere else, for they were employees of the industry rather than the firm. Ports had what seamen called the 'Pool', an employment office maintained collectively by the shipowners which was where 'owners and seamen went when looking for crews and ships respectively.

At any time after the Second World War until the mid-1970s there were only the odd months when a seaman would find it hard to get a job. There was therefore no pressing reason for a young seafarer to stay in the ships of one company, especially since for ratings there was little promotional ladder worth talking about. With a ready availability of ships and a complete spectrum of trades and world regions to choose from, it was an entirely normal thing to move around and be apparently footloose. Later, and if you had decided to stay at sea, you could always decide to settle with the firm or trade of your choice, because such was the turn-over of labour that there was always a string of vacancies in every type of ship. By 1985 almost half of all ratings were contracted to one firm in the same way as officers. For those without a company contract there is a roster system at the Pool as seafarers wait their turn for a ship. ABs can expect to wait twelve months and cooks, stewards and motormen for nine months – and the job, when it comes, may last only for several months. As for the young people, the shrinking of opportunity has been extra-ordinary. The number of new entrants as boy ratings in 1983–84 was 274, compared with 1,745 only four years earlier in 1979–80.

The typical officer had much less experience of a variety of trades and shipowners compared with the average rating. Move-ment between employers was restricted to the early years of being an officer: promotion was largely a matter of seniority, and only the most desperate tramp company would appoint an outsider to a senior rank. Such movement as there was at senior levels was mainly confined to engineers. They had transferable skills much in demand for management jobs in such places as power stations and shipyards.

Acute officer shortages in the mid-1970s saw a great deal of untypical movement of middle-ranking officers as they saw opportunities to move quickly up the promotion ladder but this phase lasted only a year or two. In the liner and tanker companies there had been an atmosphere of order and stability. High turn-over meant that promotion was rapid, so that you might be second engineer or mate by the age of twenty-six or twenty-seven, chief engineer at thirty and perhaps master by thirty-five. Em-ployers played out the polite pretence that promotion depended as much on competence as on seniority. This enabled them to believe that they could pick and choose and the newly appointed chiefs and masters to be convinced of their own merit. The practice of the meritocratic fiction meant that the only seniority lists were those carried in oral legend. Once established in a company, the ambitious officer had to listen carefully and over a period of years before he could be reasonably confident of his standing.

Questions of who stands where no longer have the same intensely speculative interest. Successive rounds of early retirements, voluntary redundancies and then the final indignity of compulsory redundancy have eliminated any sense of predict-ability and progression. Thousands of officers from what were once regarded as impregnable companies have lost their jobs.

Some, in terms of youthful expectations, have traded down into coasters and offshore supply boats, while others have gone off to work in foreign-flag ships. A measure of the future are the entry statistics. In 1984 there were 163 new deck and engineer cadets, compared with 1,800 in 1979–80. Little wonder that in the summer of 1983 the officers' union produced a campaigning leaflet with a photograph of a red ensign and superimposed over it the slogan 'Take a good look. Soon you might not get the chance'.

References

1　F. T. Bullen, *The Men of the Merchant Service*, London, 1900, p. 1.

2　P. Fricke, *Seafarer and Community*, London, 1973.

3　R. Schrank, ed., *Industrial Democracy at Sea*, Cambridge, Mass., 1983.

4　The most recent additions are: A. W. Kinghorn, *Before the Box Boats*, Emsworth, 1983, and Cedric Best, *Project Master Mariner*, Lewes, 1984.

5　R. Hope, ed., *Twenty Singing Seamen*, London, 1979; R. Hope, ed., *The Seamen's World*, London, 1982; R. Hope, ed., *Sea Pie*, London, 1984.

6　Good examples are: *Sea Way Only*, London, 1937; *The Commander Shall*, London, 1938; *Anchor Comes Back*, London, 1939.

7　From a longer list: *Between the Tides*, London, 1939; *Hollow Sea*, London, 1938; *Broken Water*, London, 1937.

8　R. Hope, ed., *Voices from the Sea*, London, 1977.

9　For a history of Straits Steam, see: H. M. Tomlinson, *Malay Waters*, London, 1950. For some reminiscences of masters sailing in Far Eastern feeder trades, see: Charles Allen, *Tales From the South China Seas*, London, 1984, ch. 8.

10　There is a good evocation of life aboard this type of ship from the officer's viewpoint in Kinghorn, *op. cit.*

11　P. M. Heaton, *The 'Redbrook', a Deep Sea Tramp*, Pontypool, 1981. For an extraordinarily similar voyage in the 1880s, see: A. Hurd, *The Triumph of the Tramp Ship*, London, 1922, pp. 175–9.

12　*Lloyds List*, 5 February 1985. For a general account of ship types and voyage patterns, see: A. D. Couper, *The Geography of Sea Transport*, London, 1972.

13　For tanker life, see: S. J. Harland, *The Dustless Road*, London, 1973, and L. Walmsley, *Invisible Cargo*, London, 1952.

14　There are many celebratory books on the life of the passenger ship. Among the better ones are: Sir James Bissett, *Tramps and Ladies*, London, 1960, and P. Padfield, *Beneath the House Flag of the P&O*,

London, 1981. A rather different view from the 'lower deck' is in Robin King's documentary in social realism, *No Paradise*, London, 1955.

15 See: O. G. Spargo and T. H. Thomason, *Old Time Steam Coasting*, Wolverhampton, 1982. For a contemporary account of coastal bulkers, see: D. Tinsley, *Short-sea Bulk Trades*, London, 1984.

16 For the owner-captain in coastal sail, see: R. England, *Schoonerman*, Harmondsworth, 1983. For a family-owned coaster firm, see: Tom Coppack, *A Lifetime With Ships*, Prescot (Merseyside), 1973.

17 For a general discussion on the survival and significance of the large family firm, see: J. Scott, *Corporations, Classes and Capitalism*, London, 1979.

18 See: E. W. Paget-Tomlinson, *Bibby Line: 175 Years of Achievement*, Liverpool, 1982.

19 For a discussion of these developments and their consequences as well as a sympathetic account of life on the giant supertankers, see: N. Mostert, *Supership*, London, 1973.

20 *See: R. P. Carlisle, Sovereignty for Sale*, Annapolis, Maryland, 1981.

21 The best and most recent study of flags of convenience is the National Union of Seamen's *Flags of Convenience*, London, 1981.

22 The most recent and detailed analysis of British shipping is the National Union of Seamen's *British Shipping: Heading for the Rocks*, London, 1982.

23 For detailed and basic information on modern ship operation, see: P. M. Alderton, *Sea Transport*, London, 1980. For more substantial analysis, see: H. Ludwig *et al.*, *Twenty-five Years of World Shipping*, London, 1984.

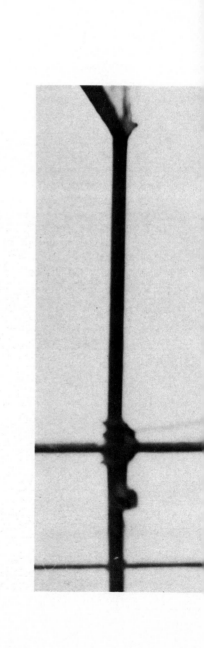

[II] · *Seafarers*

I don't know what brought me here,
Stumbling over the waves,
Brushing the wind apart with my travelled eyes,
Legging strangely on the merchant deck,
Then lying sideways in the night,
Buttressed to the rolling dream
By knee and elbow.

Some time ago, it seems,
I must have turned a corner,
And found the endless track ahead
Across the sea:
Some time ago, it seems,
I must have humped a bundle,
Said goodbye to some one and some place,
And smiled – and not looked back.

Brian Dornton Duff

I

One hundred years ago much of Britain's internal trade was shifted around the coasts in small sailing vessels. These ships were owned and often built in a hundred and one small town and village ports which were the birthplaces of most seamen.

In the twentieth century seafarers have increasingly come from the port towns and cities. The improvement of road transport services all but finished the coastal trade except for the long-distance movement of low-value bulk cargoes. Swept away with the decline of the coastal fleet was the easy opportunity for the lad from Maryport or Whitstable to start on a local boat and then graduate into the deep-sea trades. For many decades now it has been Merseyside, Tyneside and Clydeside, in that order, which have provided the seagoing labour force.[1]

These regions, in turn, have drawn their seafarers, except officers, from the densely populated terraces and tenements of the working-class districts close to dock and river. The engineer officers, usually from a skilled working-class or lower middle-class background, came from the more spacious terraces and the inter-war semi-detached estates. Deck officers, mainly from a broad spectrum of the middle class, came from the suburbs and hinterlands of the city ports.

Despite the differences in class background and the consequent variations in seeing and thinking about the world, it is nevertheless a common thing to find that regardless of class it was often a short step from growing up next to ships to sailing in them. It is the accident of birth which decides who goes to sea, in what rank and with what opportunities.

As in so many other occupations, the most common influence among seafarers on their choice of job was family. We can see this in a series of examples of seagoing careers which began at different times between 1935 and 1975. The first of these is Billy Kerrigan, a bosun until he retired: 'I *wanted* to go to sea. My own father was a ship's fireman and he died when I was about thirteen. I remember my mother, God bless her, taking me down to Moss Hutchinson's office when I was fourteen. She had with her all my father's discharge books with an elastic thing around them, and she asked to see Mr Whelan, and I suppose she pleaded for some consideration for me on my father's service. And so I got a job as galley boy for thirty shillings a month at the beginning of 1935.'

Fifteen years later, in 1950, Tony Casson, who is now a bosun with Ocean Fleets, went off to sea as a deck boy: 'My father had always been at sea with different companies. When I left school I went to serve my time as a cooper in Port Sunlight but I only did twelve months of it. I just wasn't suited for indoor work, and then, I'd always wanted to go to sea.

'When I joined my first ship I wasn't a complete stranger to ships, because I used to go down and meet my father. He was on the old *Nestor*, the passenger boat that used to come up to the landing stage. We used to go over and stay aboard her and have a look round. And then of course in those days when you went down you didn't just see one passenger boat. You'd see them all tied up down there. We used to go aboard them all – you see, my father knew everyone.'

Tony Santamera, chief cook on the Sealink ferry *Manx Viking*, which runs between Heysham and Douglas, first went to sea in 1960 from even more compelling circumstances. 'My whole family went away to sea – it was the sort of thing we all did.' (Tony has a brother who is a chief engineer and another who is a cook.) 'I followed my father and my uncles and whatever. My father had given it up about five years before I went away, but he was working in sea-related trades. There was the travel, and right back as far as I can remember there was always sea-talk. There would be parties in the house, and they were always seamen who came, and then people would drop in who'd just come back from a trip, and then there were always letters coming in. All we ever heard in the house was about ships and the sea, and I didn't know anything except ships and docks. My father often used to take me down to the docks and on to ships that he was on, and then I would go on his mates' ships too.'

Tommy Keefe is another chief cook on the *Manx Viking* and he started at sea in the 1970s. 'Tradition. It's a family tradition. My father went away and his father went away and then my older brother goes away. When I was young I couldn't see anything else except going away to sea. On my very first trip I forged my birth certificate to get a job as a laundry boy on an *Empress* boat. When I got home they found me out and kicked me off. I was fourteen then, and after that I worked on the river for twelve months – as a fireman down below, believe it or not. She was the last coal-burning tug in Liverpool. It was hard going but it was all right. But then, working on the river all that time and watching the ships coming and going ... well, it was just too much and I had to go back. So I re-entered, but legally this time!'

For these two bosuns and cooks you might say that their young lives had already been filled up with ships before they'd ever done a voyage. Others came from less determining circumstances but were shaped and pushed by the seafaring community in which they lived. Dino Livingstone, for example, had wanted to go away since he was young but had been encouraged to serve an apprenticeship as an electrician. Bored with working in factories and then redundant from construction sites, he eventually got a job on the *QE II* as an electrician and now sails as a motorman. 'I don't really know why I wanted to come away to sea, though I suppose it's got a lot to do with growing up in Liverpool, and there you can't get very far away from it. It's a seafaring community, isn't it? I suppose you've got this little B movie running through your head with this little ship sailing over the horizon.'

Then there was Peter Carney, who went away as a steward's boy in the late 1960s. He had grown up in the south end of Liverpool's dockland: 'Living next door was a bosun. He had this big map of all the places he used to go ... and then, coming from a big family with seven brothers and sisters, it seemed like an ideal way to get away from home.'

Bernie McNamee, a cook in his early twenties, is mildly surprised at where he is now and confesses to have been seduced by tales of 'good runs ashore in Brazil'. 'When I was at school and fourteen or fifteen the last thing I ever thought of was putting on a pair of checks and white jacket ... It just didn't enter my mind that one day I'd be a ship's cook. My grandfather was a seaman right through the war, and so were two of my uncles – not that that had any influence on me. A couple of the older lads I used to knock around with were talking about how they'd flown out to Brazil to join a ship and had so many good runs ashore ... Well, I was kidded by this.'

Others, while living next door to the sea and ships, were pushed by circumstance. Like Jim O'Kane, who is now mate of a coaster: 'I went to sea for work, to get a job. The town I lived in then, Coleraine, in Northern Ireland, hadn't much else. I had no great desire to be a seaman. I went to get a job. It was either that or go digging, because I didn't have any qualifications for anything else. I only went to a small school, and it was either digging drains for one of these big companies or going to sea. So I decided to go to sea.'

The same shortage of opportunity accounted for the career of an Adenese who has lived in Liverpool for many years and joined his first ship in Aden, in 1952: 'I needed to get a living. It was a job. What other reason?'

The seafaring districts have never been homogeneous. Liverpool, for example, had not one but many communities. There are still the Swedish and Norwegian churches that have their history in the late nineteenth century when many ABs in British sailing ships were Scandinavian. In the telephone directories are handfuls of Spanish and Filipino names. Still standing but derelict is the hostel once used to house West African seamen while their ships were in dock. In Chinatown are the descendants of the men who first came in the Blue Funnel ships, and until very recently a roll call of Liverpool 8's social clubs was like a tour of colonial East and West Africa. As their ships deposited them in Liverpool West Africans clung to their ethnic or national identities in self-defence and named their clubs the Gambia, Ibo and Yoruba, the Ghana, the Somali, the Sierra Leone. In Cardiff and in North and

South Shields there were comparable developments on the same theme but with different ethnic mixes.[2]

British-domiciled black seamen never experienced the same degree of choice as their white shipmates as to the type of ship and the ranks they might work in. In general they were excluded from the better-paid and regular ships like cargo liners and were obliged to work in the sort of tramps that no one else wanted. The cruder and more overt discriminations have been scarcer in more recent years, but Hermon McKay's experience of being a Liverpool-born black seaman spans most of the post-World War II period and tells a different story. He joined a down-at-heel tramp called the *Lodestone* in 1946:

'Almost the whole crew was black. It was all-Somali firemen, mostly from Cardiff, and there was one black South African down below. He'd been in the ship for years, had this feller. The deck crowd was a mixture of two Africans and two from the Caymans, one of them was a relative of ours. The bosun named McLean, he was a Caymanian too, and they are real sailors. The second steward was a Cardiff-born black lad. Then there were two Africans from Cardiff. The carpenter was a Malay and so were two of the ABs. The cook was a Somali.'

Once established, the domiciled black seamen became the tightest of all the seafaring communities, because, unlike their white counterparts, they could not so readily move into other port industry jobs. There were hardly any black dockers, firemen, warehousemen, lock gate keepers, tug men – all occupations full of ex-seamen. Most black people, once embarked upon a seagoing life, rarely knew any other. Only from the mid-1960s through to the mid-1970s, when there were crew shortages, did black seamen begin to experience widening job opportunities at sea. Hermon McKay explains the changes:

'It was strange to see a black person on certain ships, and if you saw them you'd say to yourself, "How did he get there?" But it's not strange now, and I'll give you an instance. Only last Monday (July 1983) I was coming out of Eastham locks and we're in the small lock, outward bound to the dump. I'm sitting on the after end with the second engineer and we're having a blow because it's hot down below and we're watching the traffic.

'In the big lock is one of Shell's coastal tanker fleet, and they're bloody good numbers those. It's home-from-home, and they're not easy to come by. On those it's mostly company's men and it's mostly white. But there, lo and behold, is a Somali lad forrard who I knew, and there on the after end was another Somali lad who I'd only been talking to a few days earlier in the Alexander pub. I gave him a shout but I was wondering how he'd got on that ship. My immediate explanation was that he could only be there as a holiday relief. But even so it would have been unthinkable not so long ago for them to have had that job. Particularly for a Somali, never mind me! For an African or Arab seaman to be on deck on a ship like that ...

'It was only in the late '50s that the likes of myself could get into say Cunard or the *Empress* boats. Particularly for a black feller like me, there was *no* chance on deck. People like my brother-in-law, who's been on deck all his life, in fact still is, there was no chance for him on one of the Cunard passenger or *Empress* boats. He was on several Cunarders but they were the cargo boats running to the Mediterranean. In the later years there was no problem – but they fought for this, mind you, it wasn't handed to them. Now of course they're on the rota and they get sent to any ship. But when I went to sea it was hard getting any bloody job. Even where they didn't carry any passengers it was hard.'

All the large ports had their Sailors' Homes. Built in the third quarter of the nineteenth century in a vain attempt to keep seamen out of pubs and 'houses of ill repute', they latterly became boarding houses for the internal migrants like the Shetlanders and Hebrideans who might not always go home between voyages. Among their fellow residents in the Sailors' Homes were those without families or homes.

Ships were obvious places for orphans, and many orphanages had close connections with shipping companies or with sea training schools. The connections were natural enough, since in places like Merseyside and Humberside shipowners featured prominently in the founding history of these sorts of institution. Rodney Wilson's move out of an orphanage and into a training school was a classic route for hundreds of boys. Recently retired from Ellerman's as a cook and chief steward, he first went to sea in the early years of the 1939–45 war:

'I was in an orphanage, and they used to ask you what you wanted to do, and I said that I wanted to go to sea, although I had never even seen the sea before or had anything to do with it. I was in the Midlands at the time, in Shropshire. Anyway, I went to the *Indefatigible* then. The orphanage put me there. Then the war came on, and boys were in great demand. You were supposed to be at the *Indefat.* for two years, but I was only there for thirteen months and I was whipped away. I was fourteen and a half when I joined my first ship.'

Although there might not be so many on one ship, there were altogether a lot of merchant seamen like Rodney Wilson. Some of the orphanages, especially those in the seaports, allowed their boys to go back and lodge when their ships arrived in the UK and until they sailed again. But only up to their eighteenth birthday; after that they had to make their own way. For many young seamen that meant spending their time between voyages in one or other of the Sailors' Homes that could be found in all the ports. Others might ship out again almost immediately, and some even lived out a substantial part of their adult life on one ship. Yet others would spend regular periods in one of the Homes. It is not so many years since most of the Homes had a small nucleus of men who, having once left an orphanage, spent the rest of their life alternating between ship and Sailors' Home.

Bob Evans, padre at the Mersey Mission to Seamen, was the sort of person who inevitably had regular experience of these men who had never been able to adjust to any other life than the anonymous security of the ship. 'The sort of person who came out of the *Indefatigible* and that sort of guy? Of course we did have the sort of person you're talking about, the one who had no home, and there are still one or two of those about. That still goes on, but vastly diminished. They'd leave their trunks with you and off they'd go to sea. Then they'd come back, and it still happens. They'll give you a thousand pounds, and you'll ask them how much a day do they want us to give them, because no matter how drunk you are you don't want to go over the top. Then they'd sort of say, 'Well, make it £15 or £20.' They'd drink their way through it and then find another ship. But that isn't easy these days, to find another ship when you want one, and that kind of man will find himself in real trouble now.'

Most merchant ships sooner or later had men like these. Some carried them all the time. Ships were and remain tolerant places, and often enough in the past a captain would not care too much about who he shipped as long as he could get out on the evening's tide with a full crew.

There are some obvious similarities in the experiences of those middle-class boys who went to sea as deck apprentices to become officers and those working-class boys who went as galley boys and decks boys to become cooks or bosuns. At the same time, however, there are some absolutely critical variations in background, and these stand out sharply in the following set of contrasts. First, there is John Dooligan, who is a cook.

'Most of the people I lived by were seamen. I was brought up with ships or something to do with ships – the docks. Then as kids we used to play around the docks and sneak in and then get chased out by the police. The Pier Head in Liverpool was my playground. There used to be a line of ships which you could see looking out of our window. I was living almost right on the Dock Road. Most of my 'education' was on ships. By the time I was twelve I knew every shipping company by the colour of their funnels. And when I was fourteen I went boiler scaling – you had to be little to get inside the boilers. That took me on to the ships and got me thinking about going away to sea.'

And here is John Goble, who went away to sea as a deck apprentice with the New Zealand Shipping Company, one of the most prestigious liner companies: 'I'd always lived in Liverpool, and I went to school out in Crosby at the Merchant Taylors School [a well known local public school] and when I first went to school I used the Overhead Railway. Travelling that way I saw ships all the time. I must have been the only twelve-year-old in Liverpool who could identify a ship by the colour of its funnel. Seeing all this every day just coloured my views.

'My father didn't go away to sea but he did work for Elders & Fyffes, and some Saturday mornings he would take me and my brother down to Garston docks and we would go on one of their ships and have the run of it while he got on with his work. My uncle was at sea, and then, I had other relations who had been to sea in the past. You can see that everything around me was to do with ships, and I never seriously thought of any other career.'

In the next set of contrasts there is, first, Frank Fearon, who is an assistant steward and went to sea at sixteen as a galley boy, '... the reason being that my father was a seaman, my grandfather before him was a seaman, and it just ran in the family. I started off as an apprentice joiner for six months but I just didn't have the interest in it, so off I went. Being a joiner just wasn't in my blood! My father had been in the engine room down on the coal burners. I wanted to go on deck myself – with tattoes and all the he-man stuff – but my father said the easy number was on the passenger boats, so that's where I went mostly.'

Jack Isbester, now a master, went to sea from perhaps even more compelling circumstances – but he went as a deck apprentice with the Clan Line: 'My grandfather and my great-grandfather were sailing ship masters, and my father, though a schoolmaster, had a lifelong interest in ships. He took me and my brother to London to see the *Pamir* when she lay in the London docks after her last grain voyage; we visited the *Discovery* when she lay alongside the embankment .... Captain Davie Sinclair, one-time commodore of Currie Line, was a lifelong friend of my father (they were both born in Shetland) and I recall being taken to visit his ship. Besides this, all my childhood holidays were spent on the Pembrokeshire coast, where my parents had a holiday home and where my brother and I developed a love for the sea and boats.'

In a third contrasting set we have, on the one side, Billy Kerrigan and Tony Santamara – both with ex-fireman fathers and both having family connections used on their behalf to get them jobs as galley boys. On the other side we have Captain Len Holder, who started as a deck apprentice with the Blue Funnel subsidiary, the Glen Line: 'My mother's brother had been to sea with Turner Morrison's, an Indian company, from round about 1914, and so, yes, there were family connections in that way. I was aware of this, and then my great-grandfather had had his own four-masted barque that he sailed to the Far East out of Ipswich. So on my mother's side of the family there were those seafaring connections. All through that part of my childhood I had in fact corresponded with my uncle, who later became Director of Marine for Malaysia. My grandfather was friendly with the Glen Line choice pilot. He was aware of my academic performance and that I wasn't a bad hand in a small boat and, putting the two together, decided to recommend me to Alfred Holt's, the Glen Line parent.'

These contrasts have not been artificially constructed. Without exception, all ten of the senior deck officers interviewed for this study came from middle-class families, and all except one of the ten bosuns and cooks came from waterfront working-class districts. The bosun who was an exception was the son of a small farmer. The only characteristics held in common across rank are family connections with the sea and ships – but they are realised in quite different ways. Jack Isbester visits a ship as the guest of the commodore of the line, while John Goble goes with a father who is a manager of the company that owns the ship ... Tony Casson and Tony Santamara go aboard into the crew quarters and mingle with their fathers' mates, who are ABs and bosuns, donkeymen and firemen. Jack Isbester's school holidays were spent in the family cottage by the sea and mucking about in boats, while Tony Santamara was illicitly foraging in Liverpool docks for brown sugar to mix with bicarb. to make toffee.

When it came to introductions into the world of work, Billy Kerrigan's mother had her dead husband's discharge books bound together with an elastic band; Len Holder had the Glen Line's choice pilot. Perhaps the most poignant contrast is between John Dooligan and John Goble. They could both put a name to the funnel colours they saw in the port, but while the one crawled into ships' boilers to scale them at the age of fourteen, the other commuted to a public school.

It should go without saying that these background differences and circumstances of childhood say nothing whatever about the essential characters of these men. John Goble no more chose his parents than John Dooligan picked his. When ten middle-class boys end up as senior officers and ten working-class boys end up as bosuns and cooks it is reasonable to suppose that individual will and choice have little to do with the outcome.[3]

Those who have followed each other through successive generations to become cooks or ABs or motormen, from places like Liverpool and South Shields, have been unwittingly but intensively prepared by their social and physical milieux for their rank. In the first place there has been an environment of ships and ship-related things. More important have been the experiences of family, of the families of friends and of neighbours. In the waterfront districts *everyone* had connections with the sea and ships. Everybody, furthermore, was a cook or a steward, an AB or a motorman; nobody was a mate, and very, very few got the sort of apprenticeship that made becoming an engineer, although

Tony Santamara's brother was one who did. Among those who knew most about ships, had some connections in the shipping world and were in a position to help the young, officer occupations were not so much dismissed as jobs that 'people like us do not do' – they simply never appeared as possibilities.

People born into the seafaring communities were almost 'predestined' to be what they became, regardless of their talents and potentialities. Once aboard ship the horizons of expectations and knowledge of chances might expand. The galley boy could become a cook who, if ambitious, might then become a chief steward and wear an officer's uniform. But few ABs, despite opportunity in principle, would become mates and masters, and the progression to engineer from motorman was all but impossible.

In general, the ABs who did become mates and masters came from downwardly mobile middle-class families and from such rural coastal places as Anglesey, Island Magee near Larne, the Shetlands and Hebrides and maybe Arklow in the Irish Republic. These were outposts of one form or another of still influential Protestantism, of small-scale independent farmers, boatbuilders, fishermen; places with a long and unbroken tradition of sending young men away to sea with the expectation that those who felt able should aspire to officer status. Those who became mates and masters from these communities tended to be suspicious of the flummeries of the grander cargo liner companies and were most likely to be found on those ships operated in the style of tramps – a style which approved of hard work but abhorred the elaborate displays of rank and status.

Just as it never occured to the seamen from the working-class districts of the city-ports to consider officer status for themselves, so did it never occur to the middle-class boy to think of going to sea as a rating. In each case there was a blindness to a status not congruent with one's own which would be renewed and reinforced by the sort of people normally associated with and the information they could provide. Colum Leggatt, now a second mate, provides from his own experience an example of the level of contacts that a grammer school could offer:

'The main thing was the kids at school. I was in a sort of community of kids whose fathers went away. One friend's father was captain of one of the B&I boats, the Dublin boats, and when we were kids he took me down to his ship. And then I was in the Merseyside branch of the World Ship Society and we used to go down for visits on the ships. We used to talk to the cadets, who would paint a rather rough but pleasant picture of their existence.'

When Colum Leggatt went on ship visits he was too young to be other than innocent of the workings of class, status and hierarchy. He could not have known that his grammer-school teacher, naturally and unthinkingly, would arrange for him to meet young seafarers of equivalent status. But when decision time came to him, these fleeting and arranged contacts with cadets and the spontaneous associations with the sons of captains inevitably led him in their direction.

The progression from middle-class family through middle-class school to officer status is rather like an arranged marriage. And yet things had not always been that way. The role of the merchant ship's deck officer had not always been reserved for the sons – and latterly a few daughters – of the middle class. In the nineteenth century large numbers of officers had started as ABs. By the 1920s, however, the practice of recruiting trainee officers as apprentices or cadets was widespread, and the costs to a boy's parents of an extensive kit of uniforms and other clothing, and sometimes a premium, was enough to keep out all but a handful of working-class boys.[4] It is interesting to note, by way of contrast, that Germany and the Scandinavian countries never adopted the officer-apprentice/cadet system and in these countries today, as in the past, all boy seamen start with an equal status.

In the British context it is surely significant that only among engineers officers were working-class origins predominant – or were until the 1960s, when shipping companies began to recruit engineer cadets direct from grammar schools. Until the 1960s almost all engineers had served an apprenticeship in the engine shops of shipyards or elsewhere in heavy engineering but in other respects had been influenced by the same factors as all other young seafarers. John Pritchard, now a chief engineer and the son of a foreman patternmaker at the Cammell Laird yard in Birkenhead, is a case in point:

'In the beginning it really boils down to family, because the family had been steeped in the traditions of the Royal and Merchant Navies. My great-grandfather and grandfather were

both in the RN full-time, and then my uncle became a master
mariner in the Merchant Navy. Ships were on my mind all the
time when I was a kid because I used to go on board my uncle's
ships when I was young. At that time he was a 'middie' in Blue
Funnel, and when I went aboard I was excited by seeing all these
chappies running around and the nice smells of Chinese cooking
drifting through the ship from the galley. For me there was a sense
of adventure, but a sense of bewilderment too.'

John Pritchard deliberately embarked upon his apprenticeship
with the intention of going away to sea as an engineer, his
ambition to go as a deck apprentice being frustrated by his eye-
sight. Among his fellow apprentices it is unlikely that there were
many others who had the same object in view. Shipyard apprentices could hardly fail to notice, however, that large numbers of
those who completed their time each year went off to sea. They
might also find themselves working alongside men who had
spent a year or so at sea, and among staff and supervisory workers
there were always men who had got their second's and chief's
tickets before taking shore jobs. In the shipyards, especially, the
apprentice might acquire the knowledge of the possibilities of a
career that offered promotion, and this could be attractive to
those who came from socially aspiring families. Engineers, nevertheless, did come from quite different social circumstances to the
mates and other crew members – and with interesting consequences for the shipboard status hierarchy, the subject of a later
chapter.

II

To live on ships and the sea is to be *different*, and seafarers are
very conscious and vocal about being 'a race apart', although it
is never exactly clear what they mean by it. This is partly because
seafarers have inadequate knowledge and experience of other
isolated workers to make rich and well packed comparisons. It
is also because seafarers of different generations, but members
of the same crew, have lived through different sets of formative
experiences and have come to different definitions of themselves
as seamen. There is, however, one strand in the seafarers' aware-
ness of their own history which has remained remarkably constant, and this concerns the part they played in two world wars.

Anyone who has gone away to sea since 1918 has sailed with men who were at sea during either or both of the wars and has learned, in the course of initiation, about the contribution made by merchant seamen. What they have been told is almost a literal paraphrase of a passage in C. B. A. Behrens's official history of the Second World War: 'Though the point could not be proved, it seems not unlikely that a quarter of the men who were in the Merchant Navy on the outbreak of war, and perhaps an even higher proportion, did not survive until the end ... Nothing of this sort, it seems, can have been experienced in any Fighting Service considered as a whole.'[5] Seamen have told this story more simply – that you stood a far higher chance of getting killed in a merchant ship than in any of the armed forces. What is interesting about this is that *every* seaman knows it and that the story is now passed on by men who started at sea long after the war was over. Such a continuing insistence on remembering and passing on what is now an historical statistic suggests that this story stands for something that seafarers strongly believe about themselves. The hidden meaning is not hard to find, for in the wake of the Falklands adventure, and in referring to the part played by merchant seamen, the *Daily Telegraph* spoke of merchant shipping as 'the fourth arm of the state'.[6]

Seamen of all ranks strongly believe that they work more for a service than for an industry – and they have frequently been encouraged in this over many decades. Although he characteristically forgot the existence of ratings, W. A. Coombs, an ex-ship's officer, touched the nerve precisely when he wrote in 1925 that the 'Captains and officers of Britain's merchant ships' were the 'keystone of empire' and was doing no more than echo the then Prince of Wales:

The gallantry and endurance of the personnel of the Mercantile Marine can never be effaced from the annals of Empire. The present generation of seafaring men will die knowing that they not only upheld the traditions of our forefathers, but that they also enhanced these traditions. I am confident that the coming generation will see to it that the British Mercantile Marine remains secong to none.[7]

As we shall see in a moment, this confidence was wholly misplaced, but in the meantime we should notice that, symbolically at least, the Prince of Wales did what he could. In 1928 he adopted the title 'Master of the Merchant Navy and Fishing Fleets'. He retained the title on becoming king in 1936, and the title has thereafter been adopted by successive monarchs.[8] It was through this symbolic device that the shipping industry was elevated to become *formally* the Merchant Navy. The title stuck, and in the Royal Navy there is a well established practice of condescendingly looking on the Merchant Navy as a sort of half-brother by the use of the diminutive 'the Merch'.

Other symbols and other rhetorics confirm the shipping industry as different. An Order in Council of 1918 laid down a regulation uniform for ships' officers which differed from that of the Royal Navy only in its use of insignia of rank, and the purpose of this was to provide '... a recognition of the services rendered by the Merchant Navy to the Nation ... and of the important part they play in the National life at all times.'[9] Together with an appearance at the Cenotaph each year alongside the armed services, the Merchant Navy appears in the rituals and rhetoric of patriotism in a manner not given to other industries.

It was said of merchant seamen that in World War I 'At the peril of their lives [they] have fed our workers, our wives and children; have carried the armies of democracy over sea; have supplied those armies with the munitions of war'.[10] It was in recalling words of this kind and the sentiments of the former Prince of Wales that Admiral of the Fleet the Earl of Cork and Orrery wrote in 1944:

It is easy now to say, as has been recently, that any reduction of what has been gained during the war, and any return to former conditions will not be tolerated ... This is what we all hope to be the case, but it is as well to bear in mind in this connection that everything that has been said during this war as to the debt of gratitude the Country owes to its Merchant Seamen was also said in the last war, during which every verbal tribute was paid to them.

Yet they were allowed to go through a terrible time ten years after that war ended, and there was no National cry for justice to the seamen, no movement to ameliorate their hard lot.

They were forgotten.[11]

Sentiments in this same domain are embedded in the thinking of men who were at sea in World War II. Without any prompting at all, Billy Kerrigan offered this obviously oft told (and accurate) reminiscence: 'I think it was the *Athenia*, a Donaldson-Anchor

Line boat that was the first ship torpedoed in the war. The survivors were met by the Queen Mother, who told them that without them there would never be an England.'

This memory and many similar, laden with the same sentiments, has become part of the folk history, part of the inheritance, of young seafarers, and it helps them to sustain two sets of beliefs about themselves. On the one hand the fragments of handed-down history combine with the quasi-military hierarchy of the ship to produce a *service-like* ambience and encourage the view that their work produces values superior to those of commerce. On the other hand the tales told of the celebration of wartime sacrifices and peacetime indifference help to sustain among *all* seafarers a sense of solidarity in the worth and value of their occupation. Perhaps it is the solidarity of the slighted and the ignored that encourages seafarers to think of themselves as a race apart.

It is not only a sense of history that makes them aware of their isolation. There is also the fact that being away for long periods makes it hard to maintain the networks of friends and acquaintances that other people take for granted. Tony Hinks tells his version of a story that every seafarer has told at some time or other: 'Lads coming into the game have got to understand that it's a lonely life. When you're at home all the time you've got friends and you've got acquaintances but when you go away to sea you lose your acquaintances and your friends become acquaintances. I came home a fortnight ago and walked into the pub and everyone says they haven't seen me for a long time and when am I going back! The first bloody question they ask is when are you going back! Ten minutes later someone comes in who they haven't seen for two weeks and they've got more to say to him than they have to you.'

This typical experience is more keenly felt now that there are many fewer seamen than there were, and the waterfront districts no longer densely populated with all those people whose living depended on repairing ships, loading and discharging ships, provisioning ships and then giving them their sons to be seamen as they in their previous turn had also been given. The overlaps and interdependencies between workplace and place of residence have disappeared. The seafarer home from the sea can no longer drop in on any one of a score of pubs and find it overflowing with men off the ships for a night or home for a few weeks.

Shipboard life might be even lonelier. Rodney Wilson says of the container ships, 'You can be sitting in your cabin when a feller comes down off watch and all you hear is the hiss of a can being opened and then a bit of music.' An eloquent observation which is echoed by Padre Bob Evans: 'I think perhaps the modern ship has produced a new kind of loneliness among seafarers. You can be on the bridge for an hour or so in front of your console and not see another guy. Then there are fewer of you aboard ship. I mean, what's the average crew on, say, a 50,000 tonner − twenty-five or so? By the time you've been divided into watches and had your sleep the chances of actually meeting a shipmate are much reduced. When you're handing over watches might be just about the only time you meet anyone. And then when you're in port it's almost a case of all hell let loose, isn't it? There isn't time to stop and stare, to have a good scratch, to talk. And there isn't all that time in port. And then our dock systems have gone mad, haven't they? No longer is the quayside up against Woolworth's, and then if you're tucked up against the west wall at Seaforth it's in outer space. It's a mile and a half before you see another human being, and if you're docked within the container dock itself then you have to have a flashing light in a helmet on your head before you're allowed to walk through the container system. You have to wait for a bus, so you don't go ashore. So there you are, on the fourteenth floor by lift, in your seagoing can with no one to talk to.'

Father Anthony Stringfellow, of the Roman Catholic Apostleship of the Sea, enlarged on this point. 'I think perhaps the problem has got worse than it used to be. Nowadays, of course, everyone has his own cabin, and more and more of them carry their own stereos and now videos too. Then he has his own duty-free drinks and increasingly, I'm sorry to say, his own drugs too. But I think with all this personal technology there is a tendency for people to isolate themselves more than they used to do.

'On top of that, ships today have much smaller crews, and that means the men have fewer chances of being together, of even meeting each other just in passing in different parts of the ship. *This* aspect of the problem has even been officially recognised – naval architects and shipowners are now thinking of ways of designing the accommodation so that in the normal course of moving about they can ensure that people have a chance of meeting each other.'

The loneliness that these two men see as they look in from the outside is real enough. But numbers and crowded fo'c'sles or cabins with two, four or six men to them did not necessarily mean that the ship had an active social life where everyone could confidently feel at home, supported by and supportive of their shipmates. Barney Moussa, a Zanzibari who has sailed out of British ports on British ships since 1943, tells a very telling tale.

'I was on a ship once called the *Mariante*, a London Greek, and the sea was so nice in the Pacific. We had come from Australia and the chief steward was in the bow there watching the porpoises diving and weaving ... and then suddenly at twelve o'clock somebody saw the chief steward jump overboard ... And I wonder, if it's so romantic why did he jump overboard? Maybe he was thinking, "Why didn't I get a letter last port?" because a letter means everything to a seaman. As you know, as soon as a ship gets in port every seaman goes to the messroom to see if there's a letter for him. And when there's no letter there for you, you are wondering what other people are saying ... If you are married you wonder why you haven't had the letter. I've seen people write a letter for themselves, they write to themselves through the shipping agent at the next port!'

Letters are the seafarer's way of nurturing a social world outside the ship and, in return, a way of receiving reassurance from it. Letters also offer some compensation for the artificial society of the ship, where it is chance, not choice, that assembles a crew. The recognition seamen sometimes give to this is in their ironical substitution of the term 'Board of Trade companions' for 'shipmates'. It is true that strong friendships might be struck and that subsequently two men, perhaps in separate departments, would ship out together for a number of years. 'Pairing' of this sort is rare now that men must queue for jobs and in any case only normally applied to ratings, who could choose their jobs.

Despite the acute anxieties and expectations that accompany the delivery of mail and the fevered scribbling to dash off a letter to send off when the pilot drops over the side, seamen develop an ambivalence towards life ashore. If there is invariably a pervasive sense of elation at the prospect of making port, even if only after a few days at sea, there is also a frequent sense of relief on leaving again. There are positive attractions in the relative simplicity of life on the ship at sea, and they are finely drawn here by Captain Jack Tanner:

'It was a way of life that I liked. You felt as though you were an abstract part of the world. You had no contact with the shore, and especially in bad weather you could feel that you were completely in charge of your own destiny.

'Then you could be glad to leave a port and, especially in the Med. in summer, you'd be looking forward to getting a bit of air in the ship. You might be in Famagusta or Alexandria for a week or ten days and the ship would start to smell – and then when you'd been at sea for say three hours the ship would be fine again. And then, of course, on leaving port you could feel that you were leaving all the madness of the world behind. You could look forward to a nice restful trip home; coming home from Cyprus, you'd think to yourself that you had eight nice quiet days. One of the things that frightened me about coming ashore was whether I'd be able to put up with the rush and the madness. It worried me. You see, I think seamen are an entirely different breed.'

The rhythm of ships' work and the division of labour make it easy for certain crew members to lead very self-contained lives. Each of the three mates on a foreign-going ship keeps a separate watch. Each of them has a different work and sleeping pattern and is accustomed to keeping the bridge watch alone except perhaps for an apprentice and the AB on lookout. With the engineers working daytime hours and the radio officer working his own shift system, and then with the taboos on social mixing with other crew members, the mates' life is bound to be a bit separate.

Mates do not seem to find this exceptional. Their officer status, middle-class background, and commitment to progression through a career, combine to give them a distinctly individualistic outlook on the social arrangements of the ship and the world in general. It is true that they will deliberately arrange social events embracing the entire crew when the ship is at sea, but this usually comes through exposure to the synthetic language of 'man management'. None of this means that deck officers have no understanding or experience of loneliness, merely that they are fairly well equipped to cope with it. This does not apply so much to engineers, for *their* work requires co-operation in teams and an explicit recognition of mutual interdependence. Other things being equal, engineers are normally much more sociable than mates. Among other crew members a premium is placed on sociability, on being a 'good mate'.

Being a proper mate, a 'good lad' is the most important personal quality, the one that gains most public recognition among cooks and stewards, ABs and motormen. What is involved in this is shown most concisely in Dave Kirkwood's definition: 'At sea now the bar's the centre of your life on the ship, because if you sat in your cabin for the whole trip you'd end up tearing your hair out. Some fellers *do* crack up. If they're not socialisers and they sit in their cabins the slightest little thing can make them crack up. A bit of bad news and they crack up because they've no one to talk to. If you're a regular to the bar, then you're classed as a socialiser and so you can take your problems to anybody because you're a 'good lad'. But if you sit in your cabin for most of the time and then you've got a bit of a problem, well, you just try telling someone your problem who's been in the bar all trip – they don't want to know. You're not one of their set. Seamen are very cliquey, you know, but there's no age limits. The main thing is who you are and how you behave. The thing to be is a 'good lad'. On shore you could be the worst feller but on the ship, as long as you *appear* to be a good lad, you'll get taken in and accepted. If you buy your round and relieve your mates on time, have a laugh and a joke, then you're OK. You're a good lad.'

Dave Kirkwood is unusually reflective about mateship. Although he is on the inside of it, he can also look at it from the outside. John Dooligan, however, who has been at sea for forty years, has absorbed it to the point where retrospectively it was the aspect of his life which held everything else together. 'I've enjoyed my time at sea. I'd do it again. A lot of fellers my age packed it in when they got married but it wasn't long before they were saying that they'd go back tomorrow. It was comradeship, mates. If your mate had a pound and you had nothing you'd both go ashore on a pound.'

For Joe Taylor, who is much the same age, it is much the same story: 'The sociability on board ship is good. You get the odd arguments. You hear some of the lads arguing, but then they get together and sort that out amicably. It's all over in a few minutes, then somebody brings a can of beer or it's "Come on and have a cup of coffee," and that's the end of the matter. There's good comradeship; lads help each other. If somebody is a bit dismal because they've had a letter from home or somebody's sick ... then the boys cheer him up the best they can.'

This theme is repeated so often that it is clear that among seafarers it is an article of faith. It is the central part of the way they see themselves. Like this thirty-five-year old cook who recently went back to sea after a two-year spell ashore: 'They're better mates than what you've got ashore, they're a different type of people. Say if you were skint and they were going ashore, they wouldn't leave you on the boat, they'd take you with them. If it was ashore and you were skint they'd leave you in the house! They're not mates.'

This celebration of shipboard mateship should not be taken too literally, for as Bernie McNamee says with a puncturing blast of realism, 'Fellers think its great to be going away to sea but in actual fact you're living that close that you can hear a man fart in the next cabin. There's no privacy on the sort of ships I'm on, and you tend to get on each others' nerves a lot quicker. One feller might say something in a joke but then you turn on him aggressively.'

Aggression, however, is usually contained, for as Dave Kirkwood says: 'We do get quite a lot of punch-ups on the poop, but that's as far as it goes and once it's over they're mates again.' Without a reaffirmation of mateship, life would be intolerable in the non-officer portion of any ship's crew, and there would be none of the social cohesion to underpin the *self*-regulation which is the basis of discipline on merchant ships. There is also another aspect to seamen's mateship. It is a way of expressing male solidarity and 'being a man'. Despite the gulfs which separate officers from other crew members, there are certain shared understandings of 'being a seaman' and 'being a man' which are held in common regardless of rank. These shared self-images play a critical role in softening conflict.

The recollections seafarers have of their early voyages as youths have an extremely important function when they can be turned and shaped to contain a description of conditions and circumstance that were resolutely endured despite the hardship.

The recollections are a representation for the narrator and the listener of what is involved in becoming a proper seaman. A classic of this type is Rodney Wilson's account of joining and then sailing in his first ship, early in World War II:

'I was in the Sailors' Home in Canning Place, Liverpool, sitting on the steps, when this feller came up and asked me if I could peel spuds. I said I could, and he replied that I'd got a 'sight' – that's what we called getting a ship in those days. He told me to go up and see Mr Hobbs and get my mattress and my pillow in the morning. Off him you got a palliasse and pillow covers, and you went down in a sort of dungeon of the Sailors' Home and you filled these covers with straw and then took them down with you to the ship next morning.

'There was this great rusty lump of iron ... then you get aboard and you see the toilets ... then you go into your room and there's only a paraffin lamp. The room was full of smoke because it had been used the night before. There was only two blankets and you threw away the palliasses the feller before you had had ... then the wardrobe was falling to pieces ... There was no bathroom. You bathed out on deck out of a bucket. All your hot water came from down below in the engine room. The hot water you got was from dripping joints or valves on steam pipes from the engine. Then you mixed that with some cold water and got some feller on deck to throw it over you. To do your washing you threw your clothes over the 'wall' on the end of a line. That was the shirts and trousers. If you left them over too long – fiteen to twenty minutes was reckoned to be the time – then they fell apart when you got them back on deck.

'Hours in those days weren't regulated and the food was disgraceful. The meat was in big barrels down in the store room, massive barrels about four feet high. I was only small then – about four foot two – and I had to climb up the side of them and fish about in the brine to see if there was any meat. If there was I had to get a hook and fish it out. Red, fat and slimey stuff it was, and I nearly fell in that barrel many a time.'

Deck officers usually went to sea at much the same age as deck boys and galley boys and in most cases a substantial part of the initiation meant that they too started with the most menial and dirty jobs and experienced living conditions not much different from the other boys'. Captain Fred Patten went

to sea during the war and in a ship that differed very little from
Rodney Wilson's:

'I joined her in Surrey Commercial Docks in London – the
Winkleigh. She was about 5,000 gross tons. She had spent a lot
of time in the East and she was absolutely crawling in
cockroaches. That was the first thing I noticed.

'This ship didn't have running water at all. She had an old
pump on each side of the galley and connected to the fresh water
tank. I remember us all coming back having been to the pictures
in London and I was extremely thirsty – I think we must have
stopped at a pub on the way back. Now in the mess, in a drawer,
we kept these great big pint pots, and so I took out this mug and
went to the pump and filled it with water. I took a great swig and
felt these lumps going down. When I went back into the mess I
put the light on and there in each mug were three or four
cockroaches all trying to get up the smooth side of the pot.

'The Old Man was a real tartar and he wouldn't dream of going
to the expense of having the ship fumigated abroad, so all the
sailors used to collect cockroaches in matchboxes and when they
were going up to the monkey island would empty them down a
vent which led into the Old Man's room!'

The way Fred Patten explains coping with these conditions
explains everything: '... when there are four of you all more or
less the same age you're not inclined to complain too much
because it would almost appear as if you were a mummy's boy.
We put a brave face on it, we liked to think we were hard men!'

The 'man's world' of the ship is strong and powerful and very
attractive to fifteen and sixteen-year olds. For Frank Fearon, we
have seen earlier, there was getting tattooed and all that 'he-man'
stuff. More generally, being the quintessential seaman involves
fortitude in hardship, taking physical risks, being able to 'take
your drink' and finally 'prowess' with women. In the case of the
latter demands for evidence in proof are the least onerous and
artistic licence most allowable, for it is here that seafarers, again
like other men, are least sure of themselves.

Yarning on one or another of these subjects is staple diet,
especially when a well-known and often visited port is only a few
days distant. As Dave Kirkwood says: 'The way it is that when
something crops up one of the older guys will say that when he
was on such-and-such this was the way they did it and then it

goes on from there. You might be going to a port where these lads have never been and then one of the older ones will say he was there in '60 and then someone else will say he was there in '48 and these lads are sitting there with their mouths open.'

Jim Slater, now general secretary of the NUS, recalls much the same scene from when he was first at sea just before the war. 'You used to listen to everything that was being said. Stories of what had happened in this port and that port, and you'd be thinking that I'm going to do this and that. I often think of some of the stories that I heard, like the two firemen when we were going from Jarrow to BA. I was on a ship called the *Kingsbury* at the time, one of Capper Alexander's that was bound for Buenos Aires ...: and I remember that we went looking for the donkeys that the two firemen had been talking about. There was some bar in Buenos Aires where these two fellers, coming back from the Arches, were supposed to be meeting two girls but were so drunk that when they woke up they were lying on what they thought was a pillow but was in fact a donkey! They were stinking and full of fleas! There were always stories like this, and they've stuck in my mind.'

Yarning provides both entertainment and reaffirmation of what is involved in being a seaman because the stories are collective autobiography. After only a few years at sea the novice has accumulated sufficient experience to be able to contribute to the story-telling, and thereafter, in accordance with the changing environment, adds in something new and by omission deletes something old. Changes in trading patterns, in duration of stays in port, in naval architecture and ship technology – all these impact on the yarns that seamen tell about themselves at work and ashore in the distillation of their self-portrait.

Learning to be a seaman involves learning a certain style as well as absorbing the more obviously 'masculine' attributes and so *looking the part* matters a great deal. John Goble catches the mood of this with unerring and affectionate accuracy when he describes his first few days as an apprentice:

'I'll always remember coming out of dry dock that afternoon, dressed up with the other [first] trippers in our new working gear and cap. When I got up on the fo'c'sle there were the old hands with their smashed down caps, grizzled pullies and well worn dungarees while we were dressed up like dummies out of a tailor's window. I resolved then that I had to smash my cap and rough up the pullie that my parents had paid good money for!

'It was a lovely Saturday afternoon in September and I thought this was the life as we went out into the Thames. In those days people used to go down and watch the ships sailing out, and so I was standing there thinking what a big seaman I was and look at that lot on the shore there. You were really full of yourself, but the next day you were going down the English Channel with a bit of a chop on it and I wasn't feeling too happy, though I wasn't actually sick. It was a beautiful evening as we rounded Land's End, though there was quite a big sea running – and here I really was thinking I was the big seaman and quite the bee's knees. Then I was woken up at three on the Monday morning and it was at this time that I discovered that ships worked twenty-four hours a day.'

In these matters of style there would be little difference between the apprentice on his way to being a mate and the deck boy on his way to being an AB. The one was as keen as the other to learn the ropes of how to be a proper sailor. Important here were off-the-job questions like acquiring an eye for a well kept ship and what the colours on a funnel and the architecture of masts and sampson post and accommodation might signify.

Any experienced seaman, whether cook or quartermaster, would be able to say that a ship was 'one of Harrison's' or a 'Bluey' merely by the silhouette. The liner companies especially had their own distinctive liveries as well as architectural styles – to the point where on a clear day and with glasses you could tell the name of the company and/or its nationality when a ship was hull down over the horizon and only its upperworks visible.[13] These silhouettes signified a range of things important to the seaman: the ships were well-found, were heavy on deck, were steam turbine jobs or motor ships, they went to the Medi and back in six weeks or to Aussie and back in five months. They were good feeders or bad feeders; there was plenty of 'ovies' or never enough; on those ships you got two cans a day while on another you got four with the tops on. There were the company nicknames. Shaw Savill & Albion was Slow Starvation and Agony; Esso was Eat Sleep Shit and Overtime; Harrison's, with funnels with two white and one red stripes, was Two of Fat and One of Lean; Hogarth's of Glasgow was Hungry Hogarth's ... and so on.

These silhouettes, these nicknames, these colours immediately suggested answers to every pertinent question a seafarer could ever want to ask. Apart from the symbolic functions of ship recognition there was also an aesthetics. When a ship was entering or leaving port its crew would know that it was being judged by others as to the state of the paintwork and tidiness of its gear. Among the knowledgeable watchers would be those who had sailed in ships of that company, or even that ship, and they could be relied upon to provide a running commentary as to their customs.

Knowing about ships is one of the surprisingly many traditions that have been passed on from the days of the sailing ships. Only the ship names and some of the technical terms would need changing to make James Harris's account thoroughly contemporary, although he was describing a scene in the late 1890s:

They came round the corner [Cape Horn] in company with *Ditton* and *Loch Linnhe* and next day caught up on *John Cooke* and *Springburn*, both much longer out from 'Frisco than they. Ships' names! Of course they remember them, remember the name of every ship they've been in company with and can distinguish them, hull down, by some known peculiarity of rig or cut of sail. The talk is of ships; it is always of ships and anything concerning them ...[14]

This watching and learning and knowing about different company fleets and their practices and traditions inculcates a sense of belonging and a pride in work and ship. In Jim Slater's memory that pride in craft is still fresh:

'In my earliest days I can remember preparing the ship for sea was just that. You were using your hands to prepare that ship to sail say from the river Tyne to the river Plate or to Fremantle in Australia. You knew that if you didn't do what you had to do then the likelihood of that ship reaching there was reduced ... There was the constant check-up, the maintenance, making sure that when you got to your destination everything was going to work. I always used to have that feeling and never got off it of walking down the gangway when you reached port and going on the quay and just standing there and looking at the ship and thinking, "Well, we brought you here and we'll take you back and to the next port, wherever it is." You felt that *you* were doing that. You had the feeling that you had carried the ship on your back from A to B.

'Even as I developed and got older and became bosun I made a fetish of going round the ship, especially if we were going out into bad weather, of making sure that all the wooden wedges were driven home, that the locking bars over the hatches were tightened up ... and then you could watch her dipping her head into it with the feeling that bugger-all was going to shift when the seas washed over. There was that satisfaction of seeing the ship awash from stem to stern and thinking that if you hadn't done that job she'd be under the ocean.'

Attachment to particular ships or classes of ships is generally much commoner among officers, who may well spend their entire career at sea with the same company. In those circumstances a man might well sail a number of times over in the same ship and then in others identical to it. In cases of this sort the ship might come to represent a man's history, and we can see a little of this in Mick Gibbon's story of the handing over of the *Hinakura* to Taiwanese breakers in the mid-1970s: 'We were all going off in the launch and the skipper gave us a bottle of Babycham each to throw at her sides as we left. He said it was very sad and since she'd been launched with champagne why not send her off with champagne? It's a bit rough, I suppose, especially for a feller who's been years in the ship, and he was obviously very sentimental about it.'

Seafarers invariably talk with poignancy of ships going to breakers' yards, although, despite appearances to the contrary, this has little to do with anything intrinsic to the ship. Periods in the development of the shipping industry have been marked with distinctive styles in naval architecture and these have then become signifiers for seamen of different parts of their lives. The ship, in other words, embodies a part of what the men who have sailed in them understand about themselves ... the breaking of a ship is, so to speak, a destruction of part of their lives.

Today's seamen, those of them who came to the industry in the period stretching from the war to the late 1960s, are particularly prone to be emotional about the scapping of ships like the *Hinakura*. Stately cargo liners of a type first built in the 1920s and still being built in various modifications in the 1930s, 1940s and 1950s and then running into the 1970s, they represented a particular way of living the life of a seaman. Where the officers were concerned, John Goble's view that it was a 'nice comfortable number' is fairly accurate. As he says of life in the ships of the New Zealand Shipping Company, of which the *Hinakura* was one, 'You had a bloody good social life in New Zealand and, let's face it, you didn't exactly pull your finger out on any coast you went to, and then you had long sea passages to get over it. It was a very gentlemanly way of life.'

The rest of the crew did not do so badly, either, in the small, seasonal, three-ships-a-year ports of New Zealand and Tasmania. Among the ABs on ships calling at these places there was a bit of the sailoring swagger about them when they went ashore, and even the deck boy might play at being a man of the world and be quite a somebody for a week or two.

When the last of the *Hinakura*s went, an easily paced and enjoyable style of living went with them. This was the end of the smart ship with stoned and bleached wooden decks, varnished taffrails and fancy cordage on the accommodation ladder. Lingering in these and other liner-trade ships were many of the clipper-ship practices of decorative display ... Small wonder that their passing could evoke such sentiment, seen in the bathos of a broadside of Babycham.

Part of what shapes seafarers is their contact with nature, though this is not something they talk about. There is, nevertheless, the experience of being out on the ocean, and there is no such person as a seafarer who is not periodically awed by the life and moods of the sea, the light of sun and stars and a colossal red moon erupting out of the horizon. And familiarity with this daily show has little effect on the appetite. All seafarers will find something of themselves in John Goble's remarks:

'I must say that even now, after twenty-five years at sea, a good dawn in the tropics takes some beating. You see the whole sun coming up ... and then I like a lovely sunset. When you're about a day south of the Canaries it's ideal. You see the whole sun as it goes down and then there's the green flash. The horizon has a real razor edge and then you get the most beautiful colours as the sky goes really indigo. And then the night in these latitudes. The sky is so clear, and then there's the stars. You can see the Southern Cross and there's the Milky Way and you can still see the Plough up there.

'I think you'd have to be a pretty dull sort of person who wasn't moved by that kind of thing. It's amazing that when you get a good sunset the number of people who show up on the bridge to watch and exclaim at the colours and the beauty of it all.'

The same sentiments are there when Tommy Keefe says with an eloquent brevity that he has '... seen things millionaires have never seen ... there's certain things about sunrises and sunsets.'

It is the wildlife of the sea that provokes the greatest excitement, and today's seafarers tend to be protective of the ocean's inhabitants. Here, for example, is Janis James: 'As soon as you see a dolphin everyone is at the side of the ship. They always seem to have a fascination for everyone. The thing that hurts most is when we go round Dakar, which is one of the breeding grounds for the whale, and we go through these fleets of Russian and Japanese ships culling them. You can smell the whales and it hurts. You can actually see whales running for their lives and you long to put your ship between them and their hunters but on the ship you're not allowed to, and I think that spoils the so-called romance of the sea.'

Peter Carney, for whom the job itself 'has got a bit thin', and not surprisingly after a couple of seasons as a steward on the cross-Channel ferries, remains an undiluted enthusiast: 'Being on the sea is fantastic. Being on the sea is the most amazing thing I've ever seen. The power of it when you're going through storms or, say, when you're just past the Galapagos Islands when we used to go down to Australia or New Zealand. And then, just seeing some of the things in the sea. Going through by Wellington in New Zealand, through the Cook Straits, the sea was just alive with hundreds and hundreds of dolphins.

'And then there's whales, there's flying fish. You can see all that in a couple of says. That's fantastic. And then you can see the big albatrosses. All that wears off after a while, but I'm a member of that Save the Whale. I joined that because now after only ten years at sea I've seen less and less of them, they're just disappearing. Back in 1972 you could see two or three hundred dolphins at a time and now all you see is twenty or thirty at most. You can cross the Atlantic now and that's just like an empty ocean. You don't see anything in it. Perhaps a few gannets in the air but nothing on the sea itself except a few flying fish when you get near the West Indies.'

Among seafarers there is an ambivalence about nature and what are the proper sentiments to have about it. Asked direct, they will admit to being moved by the arrangements of sea and sky and the forces that propel them, but these are not things that get talked about in the messroom or saloon. Bill Kerrigan attributes it to egalitarianism, to a feeling that an expression of wonder and delight might be interpreted as a claim to superiority: 'I think it's because he doesn't want his shipmates to think he's high-and-mighty. The seaman likes to think that he's at the same level with everyone – but he does appreciate those things, you know.'

Yet while this is convincing there are other facets to the reticence – like the knowledge that a threatening and chaotic sea can follow the most dazzling of technicoloured sunsets, and it's a long way from the deck of the ship to the bottom of the ocean, and that ships still sink without trace. And then, superimposed over these awarenesses, and paradoxically drawing sustenance from them, is the way of thinking and being a seaman – the quintessential male who dares and challenges by taking and offering physical risk. An excellent expression of this is in Bill Kerrigan's description of what he liked best in his encounters with nature: 'It may sound strange to you, but what I'm into is a heavy sea, a gale of wind and a good ship under you – particularly if I was at the wheel and all you can see is a big one coming right at you and you're trying to bring her up to it.'

Those who stay with ships for a working lifetime have made their adjustment to the inevitability of routine and the mundane. For these seafarers, though they will not talk voluntarily of it, there is still the exaltation of a tropical night, the school of porpoises, a spectacular landfall at sunrise. There is the companionability when chance sets up a crew and a master who like and respect each other; there is the escape from the madness of the headline; there is the clean simplicity of butting into a headwind hurtling out of a white-whiskered blue sky; there is the going ashore in a strange and exotic place when for once luck runs your way. These are, all of them, idealisations of moments cut free from the repetitious routines of work and social relationships. But here aboard ship, as everywhere else, it is the compensations that define the life.

Notes

1 For a range of interesting statistical material concerning modern seafarers, see: J.M.M. Hill, *The Seafaring Career*, London, 1972.

2 Some aspects of the history of black British seafarers are dealt with in: Peter Fryer, *Staying Power: the History of Black People in Britain*, London, 1984.

3 For a good survey of the literature on inter-class mobility, see: A. Heath, *Social Mobility*, London, 1981.

4 At mid-nineteenth century premiums of up to £100 were paid to get sons apprenticed to the successor companies to the old East India Company. One hundred years later, in the 1950s, the New Zealand Shipping Company required a premium of £50 (repaid in annual instalments) and the average cost of kitting out a sixteen or seventeen-year-old was about £90. At current prices (1985) that is in the region of a total of £800.

5 C.B.A. Behrens, *Merchant Shipping and the Demands of War*, London, 1955, p. 172. For statistical detail, see pp. 178–85.

6 *Daily Telegraph*, 16 September 1982.

7 W.H. Coombs, *The Nation's Key Men*, London, 1925, p. 3.

8 This sequence confirmed in a letter to the author from the Royal Archivist, Windsor.

9 J.S. Kitchen, *The Employment of Merchant Seamen*, London, 1980, p. 52.

10 Stanton Hope, *Ocean Odyssey*, London, 1944, p. 11.

11 *Ibid.*, pp. 7–8.

12 The mood is precisely expressed in Edward Carpenter's poem, *Merchant Seamen*, which contains the following stanzas:

I've read about soldiers and sailors,
Of infantry, airmen and tanks,
Of battleships, corvettes, and cruisers,
Of Anzacs, and Froggies, and Yanks:
But there's one other man to remember
Who was present at many a fray;
He wears neither medals nor ribbons
And derides any show or display.

I'm talking of ABs and firemen,
Of stewards and greasers and cooks
Who manned the big steamers in convoy
(You won't read about them in books).
No uniform gay were they dressed in,
Nor marched with their colours unfurled:
They steamed out across the wide oceans
And travelled all over the world.

They were classed a non-combatent service –
Civilians who fought without guns –
And many's the time they'd have welcomed
A chance of a crack at the Huns.
But somehow in spite of this drawback
The steamers still sailed and arrived,
And they fed fifty millions of people –
And right to the end we survived.

Taken from: R. Hope, ed., *Voices from the Sea*, London, 1977, pp. 20–2.

13 For a loving account of this in an earlier era, see: D. W. Bone, *The Lookout Man*, London, 1923, ch. 1.
14 J. W. Harris, *Days of Endeavour*, London, 1932, p. 99.

[III] · *Work*

Consider that after walking the deck for four full hours, you go below to sleep: and while thus innocently employed in reposing your wearied limbs, you are started up – it seems but the next instant after closing your lids – and hurried on deck again, into the same disagreeably dark and, perhaps, stormy night ... — *Herman Melville*

I

The ship's day begins at midnight. And in the modern ship with an automated engine room the only people up and about and working are the mates and ABs. The third and most junior mate keeps the eight to twelve watch morning and evening, and at midnight is handing over to the second mate. With the mate on watch is one AB who keeps a look-out up on the wing of the bridge.

The ship is quiet at midnight. Everyone has turned in except the watches now changing over, and soon there will only be three people awake if the ship is on ocean passage. The cooks and stewards have left the crew's bar, although maybe the AB off the eight to twelve is having a can before going below. The engineers are just leaving the officers' bar. The Old Man might be a little nervous if he has got a young and inexperienced third mate, so he is lying in his bunk, reading until the watch has changed, and turns out his light as he hears the third mate coming down from the bridge.

Up there on the bridge there is a background hum of small electric motors and the deeper muffled throb of the main engines. A locker door vibrates a little and unpredictably as the ship twists slightly to the movement of the ocean swell. Small orange lights, dimmed and hooded, break the darkness but not so much as to spoil night vision: ship's speed, helm indicator and compass heading are there at a glance. An occasional click says that on this quiet night the auto-pilot has little difficulty in keeping the ship's head on course.

For the second mate everything is normal and no anxious activity to anticipate. On an ocean crossing there is a relaxed, even casual atmosphere. There is no land to bump into, no fleet of darting fishing boats to weave through and curse, and a very remote chance of traffic from any direction. There is the sea and the sky, ship noises and dimly lit instruments. Outside, on the

bridge wing, especially on a windless night or if the wind is abaft
the beam, the rhythmic coughing of the main engine exhausts
cut the night stillness and you can taste the burnt fuel oil in the
air.

The third mate has called his relief on the internal telephone
at one bell (quarter to twelve) and then again at five to midnight
just to make sure the second mate's up and about and on his way.
Waiting for him in the bridge pantry is a mug of coffee and slices
of toast. The AB coming up to relieve the look-out has already
had his drink down in the crew's mess.

Talkative people at this time of day can be unbearable. The
person waiting to go below may want nothing to get between him
and his bunk. The one coming up for this graveyard of a watch
prefers solitude during the adjustment to being awake and alert
at this inhuman hour of rising. Here, Colum Leggatt is a normal
second mate:

'When I go on watch at midnight I have a standard routine. For
the first quarter of an hour I'll be having a cup of coffee and going
around checking the position and so on, and then about half-
twelve I'll go out on the bridge wing for half an hour, pace up and
down. Then I'll send the look-out down at one for a break and
when he's back at quarter past I'll start on chart corrections.
There's always a pile of chart corrections to be done – you might
get seven or eight weeks of them to do on a world folio. Then at
half-two I'll send the look-out down for his smoke-o and then I'll
be keeping a look-out while he's down. Generally you can rely
on your look-out these days. When he comes back I'll write the
log book, take an azimuth, work out the compass error, then send
the look-out down to call the watch at half-three. Once we've left
Panama for a crossing to Japan I don't expect to see anything. It's
a thirty-four-day passage, and I suppose you might just see a ship.
It drives you up the wall, to be honest. I find it soul-destroying.'

And out on the bridge wing, keeping the look-out, it might be
Dave Kirkwood, who is thinking of 'all sorts'. 'You're thinking
of where you're going to, if it's a decent port. Then you go into
your little sad moments and you wonder what the bloody hell
you're doing here when you could be at home. Then you're
singing at the top of your voice – there's some good singers in
the Merchant Navy, you know! Not many audiences but some
good singers ... Then like everyone else I've thought about what

I'd do if I won half a million on the pools – especially when it's Friday night and the ship's syndicate is doing the pools.'

On those ocean crossings across the Pacific or the Indian Ocean it is strange how when you are only a day's steaming away from port ships start to pop up over the horizon and converge when for thousands of miles you've seen not so much as a smudge of smoke. The AB on look-out perched perhaps 60 ft or 70 ft above the water might feel alone in the universe. At this height and on a clear night the eye can take in 170 square miles of ocean in a circular sweep. And it is empty. A school of dolphins might join the ship and play in the water displaced and disturbed by the wake. It might be a moonlit night and there might be some phosphorescence, and the cavorting dolphins leave 'vapour' trails. But this circus is a diversion. Out there at the end of the wing of the bridge and leaning against the venturi dodger which seizes the wind made by the ship and sends it curling over your head there is only the vibrating ship under you and the sound of the engine occasionally breaking through the embracing cocoon of swirling wind noises. Men get to feeling lonely doing this indescribably tedious job of look-out when there are no lights to se and the inexperienced report a meteor or a setting star as the light of the ship they would like to see.

Back inside the wheelhouse and crouched over the chart table, the second mate has recharged his draughtsman's pen and is doing his umpteenth correction. Perhaps it is a change in soundings in the approach to New Orleans, a North Sea buoy has been shifted to a new position, a drilling rig is now on station somewhere in the China Sea ... As Colum Leggatt says, his ship might have a world folio, a collection of charts which covers practically all world regions. It is a dreary job that has no end, for at every terminus the ship's mail is bound to contain yet another dreaded batch of the Admiralty's *Notices to Mariners*, which list every conceivable change registered by every last port and coastal authority worldwide. But entering them in is an improvement on the AB's job of staring into empty, watery wastes. Concentrating on looking when there is nothing to see can get hypnotic. Periodically the look-out gets into a brisk walking up and down to fight off the sleep that creeps up.

On the passages that intermittently take ships near to land, keeping look-out is more than an empty routine, and the second mate will not be doing a lot of chart corrections. Running from, say, Suez to the Persian Gulf, the traffic is regular but well enough spaced to enable the watchkeeping mate to talk to passing ships. In these circumstances the second mate might be someone like Noel Perreira:

'I think it's only me, but I never let a ship go past without calling him up. I always call them up on the morse, but very few of them answer on the morse lamp – they'll answer on the VHF [radio telephone]. I'm a bugger for that. I never let a ship go by without having a chat if I can. On one watch I spoke to five nationalities. The first was a German, then I had a chat with a Filipino, with an Arab, then with a Japanese, though the Japanese don't answer you very much and those that do have very little to say. Very few Russians answer you, and when they do it's usually when you're in a collision situation and you want to know what they're doing – then they'll answer you, but never just to have a chat with you on the VHF.

'The British are the most likely to have a chat with you because if they hear a British voice on the VHF they'll answer you but if it's a foreign voice they might not answer. Those that answer in morse will just give you the standard answer – the name of the ship and the name of the port they've just left and the one they're bound for. You don't get a conversation, the VHF has taken over so much at sea nowadays. It's standard practice to have it on all the time.'

These international conversations between passing strangers do not take place on all those routes where ships come together. The radio channel is always open at these converging points but only to assist in navigation. The traffic might be too heavy and visibility too poor to safely allow this pastime. Casual chatter is for those tropical regions where ships pass each other regularly but at safe distances and on predictable courses.

At one bell the mate gets his call, and so does the four to eight AB. After four in the morning when the watch has changed over there are still only two people about, although it is in this watch that the ship comes alive again. We can see this happening through John Goble's diary:

'The day starts at quarter to four with the telephone braying in my ear. I have great difficulty getting up in the morning, I must admit, and as you get older this watchkeeping is more and more of a strain.

'Sometimes the second mate is one of those loquacious characters who wants to gab away, but I'm all for the quick hand-over! I get in my corner with my Mars bar and a cup of coffee and then it takes me forty minutes and two cigarettes to come to life. Of course if we're approaching port and in heavy traffic it would be different because when you've got things to do you wake up immediately, but I'm talking about when you're out in the middle of the ocean.

'From about twenty to five until it's time to take stars – and of course you're always hoping it'll be too cloudy so you don't have to take them – I get stuck into a lot of paperwork – the crew's overtime, the stores book, the maintenance records – and this can be the most productive time of day for me. I'll have about an hour and a half at this until starts, which is usually at around six. By the time I've worked out the star sights it'll be about six-thirty and people are beginning to stir.

'The bosun will be up at quarter to seven to discuss what we're going to do during the day, and then the next thing is the handy-man appears with the soundings and I'll chew the fat with him a bit. Then the electrician wanders up to see that everything's working and he'll want to chew the fat a bit too ... So you can say that from a quarter to seven it's just yap, yap, yap! And then suddenly it's five to eight, the third mate's on the bridge and I haven't written up the log ...'

Before the mate has finished his star sights it will be light enough for the AB to joyfully leave the bridge and start putting all the day workers on the shake for a seven o'clock start.

II

With his calls finished and after a short break the AB will be back on the bridge and doing cleaning jobs – emptying the night's ashtrays, cleaning the bridge windows. Several decks below, the bosun and the daywork AB are doing the odds-and-ends type of jobs that can be done before breakfast at eight. A mooring rope needs a new eye splicing into it, the gangway handropes need renewing. None of the jobs are done now that no one likes. They come later when consciousness is more complete.

At this time of ship's day it's the catering crowd who are working the hardest. Frank Williams is a second cook on an Isle of Man

ferry, but he does there exactly what he would do deep-sea: 'I get
a call at half-six and I'm up for being in the galley at seven o'clock.
Then I tray up the bacon, sausage and open tins of beans or
tomatoes or whatever's on. Then I'll have the frying pan on, a
pan for boiled and a pan for poached eggs, and then a big pan on
for the lunchtime soup. At half-seven the breakfast starts, so then
I'm serving up until breakfast is over at half-eight for the officers.
Then I'll have my breakfast until nine, and then I'll go back in
the galley and get pans ready for the vegetables and potatoes for
lunch.'

There is not much variety in this routine, though if he were
deep-sea he would probably be knocking up dough for a batch of
bread before breakfast. At twenty-three his heart is not in it and,
like the AB up there on the bridge in the graveyard watch, he often
wonders why he spends so much of his life mechanically traying
up bacon and getting the stockpot on the stove. 'I'd prefer to be
doing something else, because I think there are other things that
I could do better than cooking. I'd like to be in something where
I could use my brain, because really I could do this job with my
eyes shut. It's not really putting any pressure on my brain at all,
I'm just stagnating.'

Peter Carney, an assistant steward, is no more impressed with
his work than Frank Williams. Now into his thirties, he says, 'I'm
getting a bit older, the job's getting a bit thin and I still haven't
achieved anything. I've got a few bob in the bank; fair enough.
But if I'm honest I have to recognise that I'm doing a job that
anyone could do. I've got no training or qualifications – it's just
a labouring job. As a steward it's just menial labour. You turn to
at half-six after the watch has called you, and then you start with
cleaning the alleyways. And then you call the officers who are
going on watch at eight with a cup of tea. After I've finished cleaning my alleyways and stairs I go and get changed into blues and
white shirt and dicky bow tie and serve breakfasts from half-seven
to half-eight in the saloon. After breakfast the other steward
would be going around the officers' cabins, making their bunks
and cleaning.'

The engine room, which has been deserted at night, now
begins to see some activity as the duty engineer goes round for
a pre-breakfast check. Mike Wake, a third engineer with Blue
Star, describes the routine:

'If I was duty engineer I'd be woken by the bridge to get below and do a check round and then hand over to the next duty engineer at eight. The new duty engineer would go round with a check sheet at sea. You start at the top of the engine room and work your way down, and that normally takes about an hour and a half. What you're doing with your check is checking gauges with their local readings against the remote instruments in the control room and then you're also checking things that aren't monitored.

'If I wasn't duty engineer the day for me would start at seven for a seven-thirty breakfast and an eight o'clock start. I get woken in the morning with a call on the intercom, usually from the duty engineer. My first job as a fourth engineer would be to make sure that all the oil tanks were topped up. In an ordinary day, and if I weren't duty engineer, I might be doing an 18,000 hour survey on a generator. Now that's a big job and involves stripping everything down. We'd work on that until smoke-o at ten, which is supposed to be fifteen minutes. Then at half-eleven I'd take a set of oil figures for the chief and knock off at twelve for twelve-thirty lunch and then get back to work at about five past one.'

Also working down below will be a motorman or two, or perhaps a general purpose rating (GP). Dave Kirkwood, though an AB by training and instinct, sails as a GP, and that means that in a four-month trip he'll spend a month of it in the engine room:

'A lot of fellers – ABs, that is – don't like working down below, and I don't myself. We call the engine room the pit, and when I was first told it was my week down the pit when I first sailed GP I was lost, I was frightened. And to this day I'm still frightened down there, because I don't know what's going on. All you really do down the engine room is keep it clean of oil, and then appearancewise you're 'sugeeing' (washing down bulkheads with detergent or a soda solution) 'and painting. Now and again, if any big jobs come up, then you're working with the engineers as their labourer – fetching and carrying and lifting. Any dirty jobs, then you do them.

'I'd do anything to get out of going down the pit. What frightens me about the engine room is the noise, the heat and the things that are moving about that you don't know about. It's the noise, mostly. I might be crawling under some bloody gigantic thing that's making a hell of a noise but I don't know what it is.

I might be under there having all these weird thoughts. I wonder what it is that's over my head and I'm wondering that if I touch something it might blow up in my face. They don't tell you! They didn't give me any training in the engine room. They just said that I was now a GP and 'Get down there'. I'm learning a few things now, but I'm still frightened, and I've been GP about five or six years now.'

There might also be a young eighteen-year old engineer cadet on his first trip to sea and no less daunted. Peter Hyde, for example, says: 'I must admit it took me a while to adjust. I had been on big ships before, but never anything as big as this 110,000 ton tanker. It was like a cathedral in the engine room; it was huge. It was a motor ship, but they had big boilers, because the cargo pumps were steam turbine. I was a bit daunted by the size of it all.

'And then there were all the valves. There seemed to be valves everywhere, and people going around and opening and closing them without any nameplates to tell them what was what. It was if people had images in their heads of piping diagrams. I'd be told what to do but I didn't know at first what I was doing. I'd just be out there attacking this mass of valves. It all seemed a bit scary, though people were reassuring me that I'd get the hang of it.

'The heat was terrific, and I got so tired running up and down ladders to get spanners from the workshop and so on. Outside the control room the temperature was up to 40°C, and that's over 100°F. You do get acclimatised, though, and since then the heat has never really bothered me. I've learned to sweat without any effort, if you see what I mean. Engineers learn to sweat without it bothering them. The thing is to drink a lot and keep your salt tablets.'

For Jim Kierans, who first went away as a nineteen-year-old fireman in a coal-burning ship to be at the Normandy landings in 1944, the engine room is still something of an Aladdin's cave: 'I love engines. Yes, I do ... if there's something wrong, then I'll know it. Engines for me are like music, but I read in a book one time that if you can hear music in an engine then you're crazy! It's like an orchestra, and you hear the wrong note and you walk around trying to think what it is, and then maybe you walk up to the second and say to him to have a look at that gennie.'

In a varied career, now nearly over, Jim Kierans has sailed on practically all types of ships with all sorts of engines. But always as a greaser, a fireman, a donkeyman or a storekeeper, the two latter being the equivalent of bosun. 'Stores' and the bosun are often the oldest members of the crew and full of pride in their work. Jim Kierans is no exception:

'Sometimes you know more than the engineers – you know what I mean? Mostly a donkey-greaser keeps watches ... The old donkeyman has a knowledge. An instinct more than a knowledge. There are things you accumulate, like hearing the right noises. You're oiling and greasing all the machinery and the main engines, so you have a knowledge of the engine room. Often when you're changing a unit you might know about it better than the engineers, and that's like any good donkeyman. And they'll listen to you. Even the chief and the second will come along and ask you what you think, and you won't think any the less of them for that. Even though they're highly trained men they'll say to you that there's something wrong with the main engine and ask you what you think.

'Even with these modern alarms you can detect things before the alarms do, because they only detect them when the damage is done. I was on one of those Manchester Liners once, and I said to an engineer that there was something wrong, but he told me I was crazy. "Look at the board," he said, "there's no alarms going." He asked me to go and make a cup of tea, and the next thing the place went mad – the bottom ends had come out and we had to shut down the engine room. The chief and the second came down and said to me that the third had told them I had detected something even when the instruments hadn't. But, you see, I'd detected it with my hand. It was the temperature on the casing, it was too warm. This was a modern ship and the alarms were triggered by gas which I wouldn't have noticed. You see, only when the temperature had built up enough to create a gas did the alarm go off.'

The engineer's ear is something they all have and recognise in each other. Indeed, to recognise it in yourself, to know that you have it, tells you and reassures you of your membership of the fraternity. The older 'down below' hands have their developed senses to compensate for their lack of technical training. The young engineer knows, however, that the senses even for a trained man confer something of the mystique of the 'old hand' that every young dog aspires to. And so here is the young Mike Wake again:

'The instrumentation is really only a back-up to your basic senses. If you're an engineer on a UMS [Unmanned Engineroom] ship you're still doing a proper "watchkeeping" job ... Even from the top of the accommodation, imagine the scene. It's nine or half past of an evening, and the film's just finished and you're sitting having a chat and a joke, when suddenly you'll see the engineers sit up straight like a dog does, they'll slowly turn their heads, their glasses will go down and they'll be running off down below – and just as they're half-way down, the alarm goes off. This sense of hearing, of knowing what sounds right and wrong, is your basic one, even before sight. There are things you can hear before you see them.'

Another of the ship's officers who depends on his ear is Sparks, the radio officer. On watch from eight to twelve in the forenoon, for two consecutive hours between six and ten in the evening, and then a further two hours at any time to suit the ship's operations, the radio officer will spend most of his time listening in to 'speakers which separately carry the voices of those using radio telephones and the ceaseless high-pitched chatter of those signalling in morse code. Although many messages are now carried by radio telephone, morse remains widely used, and the knack with this medium is learning to hear what is important. Howard Benson has had twenty years' experience, and he says:

'You immediately pick up an SOS or a Mayday ... You can listen to this thing turning out garbage all day, and then suddenly my subconscious will tell me that something interesting is going on, and then I'll concentrate. It's the same with my own call sign' (every ship has a call sign consisting of four letters, the first of which indicates nationality) ' – there could be fifty call signs being thrown out and I won't consciously listen to them but I'll pick out my call sign just as I'll pick up an SOS without con-sciously listening. Of course, you pick this up over the years until it becomes an instinct.

'You know, people come in here and hear the morse chattering away and they're surprised to find that we're still using it. Morse is far from defunct, although it appears to be slow and laborious compared with modern techniques such as radio telex. When I was in the North Sea in an emergency support ship, the *Forties*

Kiwi, I sent our weather observation reports in every three hours and I always used WT [Wireless Telegraphy] for that. I could have sent them on telex but I used WT because, if nothing else, it was a way of keeping my hand in, and then the chaps in the coast stations at the other end seemed to like it. *I* like using the key – in an age when people feel that it's outmoded it gives one a certain satisfaction to carry on this 'archaic' means of communication. The fact is – and you can hear it now for yourself – it's still very much with us. It's chattering away all the time, and that's because it fills a function that hasn't been replaced by anything else – at the moment, you see, there just isn't the space for anything else, and then WT is still a relatively inexpensive means of communication, especially where there may be language difficulties. With morse you can send in any language and get it down clearly.'

In normal circumstances the radio officer is busiest in the couple of days before arriving in port, when the ship's owners or agents want an accurate Estimated Time of Arrival [ETA], how much cash is wanted for crew wages or subs, what provisioning and bunkering requirements there might be, and so on. At other times the radio officer is providing an essential safety cover for his own ship and for any others that might need assistance. He also plays a role in the incredibly dense network of ship 'weather stations', and we can see how this works through part of the duties of the mates.

At eight in the morning the third mate has taken over, and among the things Janis James will be doing is sending in a weather report and checking through those coming in: 'There's the facsimile machine printing out a weather map of what we can expect ahead – it's a telex machine which prints out weather charts. This will tell you wind speeds, heights of sea and swell, air and sea-water temperatures. And then you can get Sat photographs as well. All the ships I sail on are designated weather stations, so I might have to send in a weather report, depending on the time zone we are in. Then, since I'm the chief weather officer on board, I'll have to check through previous reports of other officers to make sure they haven't made any blunders, and then I'll write up the fair copy of the weather log.'

Ships designated weather stations means that some time in the past the master has volunteered to collect basic weather data every six hours and radio it in to the appropriate station. Sent in from ships of many different nationalities all over the world, it is these reports that allow meteorologists to draw their charts and read the entrails of the sky. Every six hours, on hundreds of ships, there are mates coding up their weather reports in strings of digits grouped in fives: the ship's position, the wind speed, type and amount of cloud, barometric pressure, state of sea and swell, air and sea temperatures, humidity ... Janis James's weather map is a picture drawn from the work of other people just like herself.

During the forenoon watch the Old Man will wander up to the bridge. He'll have a chat with the third mate, though generally speaking the gulf between them in terms of age and experience is too great for there to be much in common. So there will be a few pleasantries, a look at the chart to check progress, perhaps a request for a revised ETA, a glance at the log book, a scan of the foredeck to see what the ABs are doing – and the Old Man disappears below again.

The second mate is the ship's navigating officer and he will be another visitor. Responsible for drawing the lines on the charts, calculating the day's run and deciding whether or by how much to 'flog the clocks' that night: on an east–west passage ship's time is constantly adjusted to approximate to the time appropriate to the longitude. It is customary to summarise daily progress at noon, and so the second mate is there to calculate the distance run, average speed, revised ETA, course adjustments to be made.

Out on deck, the ABs' work varies with the weather, the type of ship and the stage of the voyage. If the ship is a tanker on the last lap home somewhere off Lisbon and batting into a north-easterly gale, then the foredeck will be awash and no one allowed on it except in emergency. If the ship is a 'box boat' in the same latitude as Gibraltar and heading south, the condensation might be audibly running off the containers, and so there will be no painting on deck until the sun is higher. If it is one of the few remaining general cargo carriers and is outward bound, then the cargo-handling gear might be coming down for an overhaul – a sort of ritual which has not changed much in eighty years. 'You got covered in grease and shite,' says Billy Kerrigan, 'but you were happy doing it. It was constructive and there was a pride in it.'

On the outward-bound tanker the ABs wil be tank cleaning.

Once washed down with equipment controlled from the deck and any gas avacuated, the men might be sent down to dig out the sludge and rust scale that collects around the pump suctions. Deck cadets, alternating their duties between watchkeeping on the bridge and working on deck with the ABs, could be certain that they too would take their turn at digging sludge, women cadets not excepted. The tradition continues to insist that if cadets are one day to be in the position of giving orders, then they must be able to do any task given to others ... and so Elizabeth Flynn found herself sent down into the pump-room bilges at the very bottom of the ship:

'I've been down tanks, obviously, but I've never had the privilege of digging them out. But I've dug out a few pump rooms, and that's even nastier. Down there you can't crouch, so you've got to kneel down in it, and you're wearing plastic trousers and wellies. The worst thing is that horrible feeling as you kneel down and your wellies fill up with thick black oil. Then it's using your little spade to fill up the buckets.'

The merchant ship must be one of the few remaining places where people eat three cooked meals a day and where the menu at lunch is as long as that at dinner. This partly accounts for the fact that in the afternoon watch the whole of the catering department and everyone else not on watch or daywork is asleep. The watchkeepers, of course, never get a full eight hours, and they supplement a shortened night. But there is always among seafarers an obsessional attitude to sleep; there is a misplaced belief that they never get enough and that what they get could be – but hardly ever is – interrupted. All this is enshrined in the afternoon kip, and so pervasive is the custom that all noisy work is usually banned until after three and the afternoon tea break.

Up on the bridge on an ocean passage and with the engine room only a source of vibration, the second mate might think himself the only person awake. Looking through the shimmering heat and expecting to see only an empty horizon on a passage from Java to the United States, via Durban, Glen Broughton was daydreaming as usual on a hugely hot afternoon:

'The sun was blazing down and burning my back when suddenly I saw this little boat and wondered what it could be doing *here*, with the nearest land several thousand miles away. She was about two points on my port bow, so I eased the ship around.

The fellers chipping out on deck by this time had noticed the boat as well, and one of the ABs came rushing up to the bridge to tell me that I was heading straight for a boat. We were getting fairly close by now, and I could read through the binoculars a sign reading SOS and PLEASE STOP. It was obvious now that it was Vietnamese people and I took the ship around them in a circle, and I could see what looked like five grown-ups and about twenty kids. I called the Old Man but for a while was in two minds whether to call him.

'When he came up we stopped the job and took the Vietnamese on board. They had been trying to make for Australia, but their prop shaft had parted. They'd run out of water and must have died if we hadn't picked them up, because they were hardly in one of the busy shipping lanes. We sank their boat to make sure it wasn't a danger to navigation.

'Now of course anyone *could* have picked up these people. But that same morning we had passed a fleet of US warships, and because they were on a reciprocal course to us they *must* have gone straight past them. Other ships had also gone straight past them, and several had circled and dropped them provisions. But, you see, a lot of masters were under strict instructions from their owners that they weren't to pick up boat people. When I first saw them I wondered whether our Old Man had himself been given direct orders, and that was why I hesitated to call him at first. As it was, the Old Man wasn't the type to sail past them and he did an excellent job in picking them up.'

Excitements of this kind are rare enough in a seafaring lifetime, and the somnolent ship's afternoon makes it almost implausible. In the engine room there is no sun to register the day's progress. Here at least the noises, smells and artificial light are constant, and there is ample evidence of activity as chief engineers like Dario Vieceli muck in:

'I was promoted chief in an era when the chief's job wasn't the same any more. The days have gone when a chief might go down the engine room once a week. I'm a working chief. I came in with these new unmanned ships, and you had to be involved with the job because the crew was cut down to the minimum, with only three engineers in the engine room. To do the maintenance the chief doesn't have to go down there, but the job won't get done if you don't go down and give a hand.

'And then nowadays you as the chief do a lot of the surveyor's work when you're at sea or in ports where a Lloyd's surveyor is not available, though of course it has to be confirmed by Lloyd's.'

John Pritchard, likewise, feels that he is continuously under pressure: 'It's largely the change in technology that has put pressure on the engineers, and then again it's automation as well. There's so much automation today in ships' engine rooms that it's beyond the *average* engineer to comprehend it all, it really is. So if anything goes wrong you have to rely on the feller who will come down and fix it. And then there's the computers you get, especially on these container boats, to work out how to stow your cargo. On several of these Harrison container boats we used to carry bananas in containers, and these were run by computers. The computer is the be-all and the end-all of the carriage of some cargoes, and if the computer goes wrong or starts to play up, then your cargo starts to play up. These computers have to be kept in a pretty moderate temperature, but if the air conditioning plant fails, then the computer fails and then your cargo fails and then everything on your control panel starts to throw out strange alarms.

'Any variation might cause your computer to go, and then you're back on manual controls – and that's no good, because you've only got three or four engineers down below. With the old engines you could see everything happening but today it's all buttons and dials, limit switches and control circuitry ... It's part of the training of an engineer that every time you walk past a gauge you look at it, and a good engineer will know at a glance whether it's right or not. But today you rely on instruments much more. You see, today you go round with ear muffs on, because the high-speed engines have got this high-pitch tone. I've had my ears damaged myself through the noise of turbo-chargers, so obviously you don't get all the sounds – the idiosyncracies of roller bearings going, of pumps – but then, this is counteracted by your preventive maintenance.'

Ships' engineers have always had a well deserved reputation for being phlegmatic and stoical types. Today's engineers, especially the chiefs, seem to be constantly anxious and running at a pitch rather higher than they would consider safe in their machinery. Dario Vieceli is a thoroughly representative chief in his expressions of alarm at the progressive reductions in engine-room manning:

'The engine-room crew has been decimated. On my last ship we had four men down below, that's including the storekeeper. What you try and do now is just keep the engine room safe. Before, the greasers would work with you. They'd be next to engineers, some of them. In fact some of them had been at sea quite a long time and were very experienced and were as good as some engineers. The only difference with some of them was that they didn't have a certificate. Many a chief would tell you that a donkeyman or greaser was more use to him than a junior engineer.

'That's been wiped out now. With some of the older hands we might still ask them to give us a hand with some jobs, but mostly we have to use them just for cleaning. What we're concerned about is safety, and in the engine room that means keeping it clean. You see, being unmanned, the biggest risk you're taking when you lock the doors at night is fire. The other one is oil on the deck and a man goes running down and breaks a leg. You've got to keep the place clean and make sure there are no oil leaks with oil running down near hot plates and so on. Under the plates, of course, it's a losing battle to keep it oil-free. With these new engines they're all fantastic when you see them in showroom leaflets but when you get them into a ship there's oil everywhere.'

By five o'clock all the day workers have finished for the day and are getting cleaned up for their meals in messroom or saloon. The cooks have had a two-hour break after the midday meal and have turned to again at about three to start preparing dinner. So far as the quantity of food goes, seamen do well, with three cooked meals a day and with a roast every day at either lunch or dinner. Quality varies with the cook, but all ships' cooks get a thorough training and, notwithstanding complaints to the contrary, the standards are generally high. Tony Santamera, being a cook, takes a more or less justifiably dim view of the moaners:

'The thing is that food can become boring at sea and cooks can get moans at sea they'd not get at home. You see, you're hardly ever hungry at sea, and this causes problems. They complain that the food gets repetitive but they don't notice that at home they eat the same things week after week.'

Ocean passages, at least on bulk carriers, have been longer in the early and mid-1980s than for twenty years. Ships of this sort have been operating so close to the economic margin that often they are run at half speed to save on fuel. In these circumstances, and with quick turn-rounds at each end of a passage, the routine of the ship can grind with unbelievable tedium. Food, therefore, can assume a startling importance, considering that seafarers are no better known for their gourmet tendencies than any other random selection of Britishers. The point about food is that with a bit of flair and a few flourishes it can offer something unpredictable, something that breaks with routine. It is for this reason that a really good cook is cherished while one who is merely competent gets complaints he surely does not deserve.

The evening watch is usually uneventful, though that description would seem excessively well modulated if we compare it with Andrew Milligan's brief yet eloquent log entries:

1600. On bridge. Nothing to do except look at the horizon.

1700. Bosun appears to discuss day's work.

1730. Bosun leaves, having discussed work for five minutes and bored me for twenty-five minutes. (Am I being unkind to him?)

1830. Relieved by third mate for dinner. Five courses, with the main being grilled Irish ox rump steak. Glass of wine. That wine not for owner's account.

1910. Back on the bridge for another boring fifty minutes.

1930. Boredom relieved by sighting of another ship on a reciprocal course. You'd wonder how, in the middle of the Atlantic Ocean, another ship manages to get exactly on a reciprocal course.

2000. Leave the bridge in charge of the third mate.

The third mate may have a more interesting watch. Almost certainly he or she will be a lot younger than the mate and accordingly less familiar with what is to be seen. The following exuberant account from Chris Warlow carries with it a fresh enthusiasm, even though far more experienced men would also have been drawn to it:

'Talking of phosphorescence, I've seen something in the South China Sea called cartwheeling. You get these micro-organisms in the water and they appear as lights in the water. But this cartwheeling is due to the disturbances the engine noise makes – or that's the theory – and creates this cartwheeling effect round the ship of bands of light. I've read about this in *Met for Mariners* or something but I've actually seen it and it was quite brilliant. I called the Old Man because he was very interested in anything like this. He told me that he'd seen it in virtually the same place but he hadn't seen it for twenty-eight or twenty-nine years, so I think it's quite rare.'

It will be a lucky third mate who has had this diversion, not to mention the AB out on look-out who will also have enjoyed the show. But the stiff-eyed second mate who will hear all about it when he appears at midnight will be in no mood to tolerate any wordy enthusiasm. Grunted responses will send the third mate below. And the Old Man in his bunk marks his book and turns out the light.

III

On passage the ship's master is mainly an administrator. Only when making a landfall and entering and leaving port does he begin to play the part that imagination expects of captains. Getting near a port often means getting near other ships, and it is at these times that the unpredictable which might be welcomed on a passage is now a source of anxiety. Fog, of course, is never welcome, is the direst dread of all masters and mates – and never so much as when making up the English Channel. As Captain Jack Tanner put it, 'Fog was the worst thing, because that could mean you'd be up on the bridge for thirty-six hours without a break. You'd have your meals brought up to you and you never left the bridge. There was nothing worse than fog. Weather could be uncomfortable, but in the fog you could never be quite sure could happen.' Leaving port in thick weather could be even more worrying. 'I came out of Oporto once and we didn't see a thing and when you go out of there you pass within ten yards of the bullnose of the pilot station. It was thick fog, and we didn't see the pilot station, though we could hear them all talking. Now *that* was frightening.'

For all its brevity, Andrew Milligan's log of a coastal voyage from Felixstowe to Zeebrugge gets to the drama of moving a ship into port in fog:

1600. Arrive on bridge in thick fog. Radio's cackling and Flemish pilot shouting and gesticulating wildly.
1651. Zeebrugge tugs fast.
1658. For'ard tug breaks towing line at harbour entrance. Still thick fog.
1659. Let go port anchor. Footsteps can be heard on the quay, but the quay cannot be seen.

1709. For'ard tug again made fast. Anchor aweigh.
1715. Fog clears a little. Ship about twenty feet off quay.
1728. Completed tying up alongside.
1729. Commenced discharging cargo.

It is customary for voyages to end on such a flat and everyday note. All the excitement and adrenalin-driven activity is in getting the ship into a position where it is nothing more than a squat and motionless floating warehouse. In Captain Fred Patten's account of entering the Manchester Ship Canal to go up to the container berth at Ellesmere Port we can feel something of the excitement:

'We generally docked either half an hour before high water or three hours after, but occasionally we would go in before high water, with a lot of tide running behind us. What with the tide and having to keep way on as well I've come into those locks at a very good speed, so you have to give them a terrific cant and then a real good thrash astern. You can imagine that it can be hair-raising in those circumstances if something happens to go wrong below. For me, that was one of the worst port approaches, coming into Eastham lock. That would get the adrenalin going, but then there was the feeling of contentment when the ship was berthed and everything went quiet.'

A recently retired master from Ocean Fleets encountered a different set of problems in trying to get his giant Panamax container ship into Rotterdam and Le Havre in heavy weather:

'Berthing, I usually have four or five powerful tugs, but I did have difficulty in Rotterdam once when it was blowing a Force Nine gale. We had the bow thrust going [propellers mounted each side in the bow which give a lateral thrust] and five tugs pushing, and we did manage to get a line ashore. Then we started gaining, little by little, but it took us half the night to get alongside.

'Then I've had trouble in Le Havre picking up the pilot. Despite the bow thrusters, the helm hard over, one engine ahead and the other astern, I just couldn't give him a lee. The trouble was I had boxes on deck astern but nothing up front – the ship had been loaded by a non-seaman cargo planner! The consequence was that those boxes acted just like a staysail on a drifter – she just came round into the wind and there was nothing I could do about it. In the end we just had to go round and try again. I got him aboard the second time.'

Once into port the master on most ships can start to relax. It is true that customs and port officials may want to see him for a signature and a hand-out, but on many ships this chore is taken over by the chief steward, even though the rituals might be acted out in the Old Man's cabin, as in this case, told by Peter Henderson:

'One time I was in Poland, in Gdansk, and there were about ten of them in the Old Man's cabin. I had to go through every crew member's discharge book with them, and they'd go through their black book to check that none of them was wanted by them – and then the agent told me quietly that a bottle of whisky and 200 cigarettes would be wanted by each of the officials. I told him just as quietly to get stuffed but he said that I'd have to give the stuff to them – and meantime they were drinking whisky by the tumblerful. Anyway, when it came for time to leave and I was giving out the bottles and cigarettes they told me that they wanted the same again. I protested but I was told we would be delayed if we didn't do it, so that was it, because it costs a lot of money for these ships to be delayed.

'In most places they're OK. They're not awkward, provided you don't try to talk down to them. If you do you've had it, because they've really got you. You see, a lot depends on the chief steward when you're in port. Everyone from ashore comes looking for you, and so you're in a position, if you're not careful, to make life difficult for everyone else aboard the ship. They come looking for the master but you try to take as much weight off him as you can.'

The master, meanwhile, might be doing a job somewhere else to free others to do more important things, like Jack Isbester on his ship, *Rocknes*. 'In the last few weeks I have spent some hours in holds and ballast tanks inspecting them for damage for the dry dock list, and I spent a couple of hours at the top of the foremast, with the chief engineer, in pouring rain, repairing a damaged foremast light. In doing these jobs I wasn't indulging an eccentric whim, nor was I covering up for an incompetent colleague: I was merely ensuring that others would be free to carry out other equally important work.'

Shipowners prefer to have their ships at sea, where they cost less money to run. So as soon as a ship enters port a great deal of energy and initiative is used to get her out again. This puts life in port on a more demanding level than at sea: the mates because they are under pressure to load and/or discharge the cargo, the engineers because they have a deadline in which, perhaps, they have essential repairs to do. Port is not, therefore, always a place to be looked forward to, and Colum Leggatt's comments display a common attitude:

'If you asked me what my big beef is – well, I can put up with being at sea, but it's getting into port, and then you're working six on and six off, so you're not going to get a decent run ashore anyway. You're not going to get a night in port, so the prospect of getting into port doesn't excite you any more. Although it's like a prison at sea you think it might be better staying at sea because at least you're not going to cop out for a twelve hours plus. It seems to me that because there are so few people you always seem to be running from one balls-up to another. There's a sort of loyalty to the ship to keep it running rather than saying, if you were down at Ford's, 'That's my shift. I've finished. I'm going.'

Down below, in the engine room, says Dario Vieceli, 'You're always in a panic, you've never got any time, never any spare time. You're not sort of saying that you can do it comfortably. You've just got to start the job and hope that everything goes all right. Normally we do finish the job before the ship is due to sail – but sometimes you don't, and there is constant pressure on you.' In this vein Tony Hinks, a petty officer motorman on a giant RO-RO ship remembers a busy time in Jedda:

'A job that still comes back to me was when I was called at three-thirty to do the four to eight watch and then we got into Jedda at about half-five in the morning. We started pulling the piston as soon as we got in and we had the head off and on the plates by eight o'clock. By six in the evening we were still going at it, though by that time we had the piston and the head back on. We put the water on and found the cooling water was leeking, so we had the head back off, put a new sealing ring in and put the head back on. We tested it again and it was still leaking, so the head came off again … Finally we got it cracked by eleven that night ready for sailing the next morning. Now that, of course, was unusual.

'Take a normal day in port. Say you get into Singapore during the four to eight and tie up for eight o'clock when the gangs come on board. Then you do your lube oil bunkering and after that your scavenge cleaners come on to clean tanks and so on. *We* can't do this sort of thing any more because there's only me and another man. Any port you go into and no matter what the time of day or night, we've automatically got to turn to. You see, there's only four engineers, including the chief, and then there's me and a motorman.'

Work rates of this order are almost routine for the coastal sea-farers. On coastal tankers, for example, sea watches are maintained in port just as they are on the deep-sea ships. But since coasters are always in and out of port and the watch below has to be on duty on these occasions, the very routine of everyday life leads to long hours. If this tends to be especially hard on engineers, it is certainly no easier if, like Barry Roberts, you are mate of a North Sea supply boat:

'If we were in port the day would start at about seven – it might be Aberdeen, Peterhead, Yarmouth – and we've been working for Shell, which is quite a hard-running job. You dis-charge what you've got on board and then you've got your loading list. It might be pipes, containers, large ungainly lifts. It's just a pot-pourri of everything coming backwards and forwards. The ship's about 700 tons and it's basically a tug with a very long deck at the back. You get a loading list for numerous locations – it might be seven platforms, three rigs. It's usually quite an array of stuff – you could be loading water, cement, fuel. This might take about four hours and then you're straight out to the field. From Aberdeen it might be a day, say twenty-two hours to the first stop, but from Lerwick it might be only seven hours. Every-thing is on a twenty-four-hour basis, and so you might have done, say, two days out in the field where you've done five on and five off and you've had very little sleep because of the weather and then you come into port and just as your watch finishes the working day starts. But set against that is that I do four weeks on and four weeks off.

'We have three ships working for Shell, and people dread going on them; won't go on them! When you get on these you work hard for four weeks and the men don't like it. You come into port and you try and turn them to, but when they've done sixteen hours out in the field they're not too keen and you must agree with them – but you've got to keep the ship working. So you're always getting gripes. And then if you're going to move ship in port it always comes at a mealtime. And so you've lost most of your lunchtime and then you're on an hour's notice to move, so if the fellers go ashore you must know where they are so you can get hold of them.'

Barry Roberts, in his late twenties, was brought up in the liner trades and that meant that he learned very early on the importance of keeping a clean and good-looking ship. Although much younger, he is of a piece with Jim Slater: the sort of man who stands on the quay and eyes the ship up and down. But working in the North Sea and at the pace of the supply boats is death for the values of the traditionalist:

'What gets me is that the environment we work in and the turn-rounds we have, the ships are a load of rubbish. They look really bad, and that really gets me. You get the charterers coming down and saying the ship looks a mess, and that annoys me because although you want the ship to look OK up in Lerwick in winter there's not a lot you can do. What really brought this home to me was that we had three periods of sixteen days to supposedly sort the ship out – which then came down to three days in winter. We painted all the whitework on the ship and I was quite pleased with it, she started to look passable. And then you go out to the first rig and get cement pumped all over the ship! That's the soul-destroying part of the job – the ship just falls apart around you unless you get a good charter. You can keep the superstructure fairly clean but it's the hull – you're up and down quays, shifting ship, alongside other ships ...'

These frustrations, however, are as nothing compared with those of a mate of a ship working cargo in Nigeria. Those who traded down to Australasia had their tales of allegedly 'strike-happy' wharfies and those who went down to Latin America had their yarns of lunatic winch drivers. But there are no stories that can compete with those that have come out of Nigeria. John Goble's diary in the day of a life of a mate is saturated with authenticity:

0700. Dragged from my sleep by the bedside telephone, the day starts. The second mate narrates the night's tribulations. Typically he will report that around 1 or 2 a.m. the lorries collecting X.'s cargo dried up or the tally clerk disappeared or some such. This being at the largest hatch, he will have spent a couple of hours shifting some of

X.'s cargo so that a start can be made on Y.'s stuff which is the sort of rubbish that can be dumped safely on the quay. Unfortunately the only place to put X. was on top of Z., who is due this morning to collect ... and so on. Typical of Nigeria, which is the only place on the globe where you cannot unload a ship in the conventional manner, i.e. start at the top and work your way down.

0730. A quick wash and into the working garb and a quick round-up of the deck. Labour just starting to straggle on board and already looking for eating, sleeping and lavatory spaces. Growl through a chorus of 'Mornin', sah,' 'Morning, Chief,' 'Morning', Boss,' from all and sundry as the carnage in the hatches is assessed. Fight my way through a crowd of supplicants for my signature on sundry forms and documents – the Empire left a great legacy of bumph in this country.

0815. Petitioners having been dealt with, proceed direct to galley door, where order breakfast, then pantry, where make up cereal and carry to glum little hole called duty mess. Over breakfast discuss initial battle plans with third mate if we have a cadet to hold the ring on deck, otherwise we confer on the field of battle.

0845. Breakfast consumed, likewise first coffee and first cigarette, feel confident enough to ascend six decks to bridge and pacify the Old Man, who is pacing the deck purple-faced and screaming, 'Why this not done?' 'Why this stopped?' etc., etc. Semi-rational discussion follows, with ratio of sensible interchange of ideas to personal abuse varying according to Master's digestive disorders and Mate's level of tolerance.

0910. Arrive back on deck, now armed with portable VHF, useful to liaise with shore staff and third mate; unfortunately also open to mixture of sarcastic and vitriolic abuse from Old Man in his air-conditioned eyrie. Day's heat is not yet really felt and labour, being fresh, are getting stuck in. Only fly in ointment is shed not yet open despite several messages and envoys sent to beg this favour. Shed is for pilferable cargo [i.e. everything that isn't taken directly away by the receiver or is so unattractive that it's not pilferable] and we need it open as much as possible, but in the event we are lucky to have it for eight hours daily. All other hours must try to jolly along receivers who'll take cargo direct or be continually shifting and sifting to find workable cargo.

1030. Send the third mate off for coffee and a smoke. Take to the offshore side of the ship and see what is starting to come out of the woodwork. Every Nigerian knows that all the crew on every British ship have smoke-o at this time, so up loot comes from the hatches. A canoe is idling by the bow, so tell the native watchman to heave a stone or two at it whilst I shake down one or two gentlemen whose trousers are bulging with ill-gotten goods. As it is considered a bit of a game, most of the swag is surrendered with grins and abuse all round. An escalation is the drawing of a knife, and the only answer to that is a withdrawal with as much dignity as can be salvaged.

1100. Hand the deck back to the third mate and gratefully escape the growing heat to the air-conditioned shelter of the cabin for a coffee and a welcome smoke. Hardly begun on both when, glancing out of the window, see one of the derricks looking distinctly sick, next minute the VHF crackles into malicious life: 'Mate, what the bloody hell's going on at No. ..., etc., etc.' Coffee down, cigarette out and off to the scene of the crime. Turns out to be a normal catastrophe. Situation is, gang below do not want to carry cargo to the hook, they want the hook to come to the cargo, winch driver likes to oblige and knows by observation how the override button works. So the derrick is slewed over its limits and one span goes slack, wire on the winch goes slack, jumps off the barrel and retightens. This might be a long job, so set the gang to working at the other end of the hatch. Get a message to the bosun to bring the crew we have (all three of them, the other two being on night duty) and set about restoring the derrick.

1200. Every bum and stiff on the deck, deserving and undeserving, wants a beer off the Mate now, everybody reminding you of their thirst verbally or by making loud sucking noises as you pass by.

1245. Return to air-conditioned sanctuary, where hand out a couple of cold beers to deserving and/or useful recipients from among the Nigerian multitude. Have just got the necessary ingredients (cheese, biscuits, glass of box wine) from the fridge when, looking out the window, see a cheeky sod up on top of some containers removing the spare tyre and battery from the back of Land-Rovers carried up there for another port. Simultaneously see the launch approaching from the harbour side. Slam door, lock it, and down five decks and along to the scene of the crime. Launch away with two spare wheels on board. Where watchman, where third mate, Old Man now screaming from the bridge, think to myself, 'One–nil to them, sod it,' get the handyman to patch up the back of the vehicles and eventually get to my lunch. Old Man still chastising all and sundry on the VHF, so switch my set off, two officers on deck cannot control 200 labourers comprising high quotas of villains, and the wine is getting warm!

1430. After eats, a smoke and a bit of a read to restore the sanity, nearly forty-five minutes have passed and we are into mid-afternoon and time to start planning the night. An inspection of the hatch shows that there are a couple of bottlenecks developing: one is down below, so the third mate is sent down to try a little close-quarters cajoling; one is on the quay, so a quick check with the quay controller establishes that some fork-lift drivers are very thirsty. This is code for slipping discreetly ashore with a couple of lemonades from the fridge and thus effecting a better attendance at the congested spot.

1700. Heat is going out of the day, the ship is slowly but surely running down to evening tempo, even the Old Man has subsided into a low background rumbling. Amble along with the third mate to open up a 'tweendeck, a small routine task to end the day. Half-way through the operation movement of the covers stops – a hydraulic hose has burst, oil spraying out everywhere. Off to get an engineer – we'll be popular, as they are all coming up for a shower at the end of the day.

1830. It's been too late to take the planned shower before eating in the saloon, so off to the galley door again to get a meal.

2000. All washed up and clean, having been intercepted by the Old Man before showering to chew the day's fat. Agreed by both parties that acceptable progress in the unloading has been made; we part still significantly differing in our estimates as to final completion and with the unspoken assumption that morning will see us coming out of our corners spitting and snarling as usual.

2200. Letter written home and even managed to wash some clothes. Best part of the day now, have shot around the deck in five minutes flat and the second mate has the operation (and the operatives?) by the throat. Now a brew of coffee, light up and enjoy a couple of hours' uninterrupted reading to close the day.

As more and more of the major shipping routes become containerised John Goble's account of working a general cargo ship becomes less and less typical. On the 'box boats' containers are often loaded and discharged at the same time, and those waiting to be loaded are carefully marshalled in sequences by specialist staffs working ashore. On the ships that variously carry ores, crude and refined oils, gases and chemicals the mate is still in charge of loading. While each of these commodities has its idiosyncracies, not to say hazards, handling them demands little in the way of ingenuity, either practical or diplomatic.

IV

The depression in the shipping industry has prompted some shipowners to try and delegate areas of commercial decision-making to their ships' masters. Commercial management of the ship was often a large part of the master's job in the nineteenth century, but rarely has it been so in the twentieth. Len Holder describes the typical twentieth-century master as an 'ocean pilot': 'He took the ship from A to B. He might make the odd additions to the ship's log, but he was no personnel manager, nor a competent economist who could understand the business decisions that were being made.'

Today, however, part of the fashionable language in the shipping industry employs such phrases as 'being a bit of a pirate'. Translated, this means that ships' masters are now expected in certain trades to exercise a bit of guile and stealth with regard to regulations, to cut their margins fine when it comes to carrying fuel and water, so that they can carry more cargo. An excellent illustration is in Eric Knowles's story concerning the chemical carriers on which he recently sailed as chief engineer:

'On my last ship the Old Man would say to me as we were arriving at Huelva that sulphuric acid was a deadweight cargo' (freight rates calculated according to weight of cargo carried rather than cubic space occupied) 'so the more we carry the more we'll make but to carry more we've got to carry less fresh water and fuel. So he told me to try and get to Huelva with as little fresh water as possible and then we'd load the cargo down to her marks and then we'd put the fresh water generator on for the trip back to the Annaba in Algeria. With luck that would make us enough fresh water to last while we were in Annaba. And of course, he said, if we run out of water we'll buy some, because that's cheaper than what we'll get for carrying sulphuric acid. Taking as much as we could meant taking as little bunkers and fresh water as we could. Fortunately, we could make ten tons of water a day and only used one and a half, so if you weren't careful you could get there heavier then when you left.'

This chemical carrier was a small ship and, so to speak, is the type that fills in the gaps left by the big ships which tend to operate on longer charters. The men on these ships lead very erratic lives, and we can see something of this in what was happening to Eric Knowles's ship before it got the sulphuric acid charter: 'We came out of Eurimca – that's a Turkish port in the Black Sea – and we sailed down the Mediterranean waiting for orders. Then we got orders over the RT to go to Agusta in Sicily to pick up bunkers – then we sailed out for three hours and then shut down and just drifted until we got orders to steam at slow speed for Gibraltar, and it was then that we went on this Huelva to Annaba run.'

Ship chartering is usually done through a small number of 'exchanges' like the Baltic Exchange in London. It is through these places that people who want to shift a commodity meet those who have the ships to do the job, and orders are then sent by radio to ships' masters. The latitude in all this for localised decision-making is naturally limited and often comes down to working out how an extra fifty tons or so might be squeezed in if it's a small ship or several thousand tons if it is a VLCC. None of this, however, comes near to what Len Holder describes as the 'dodgy end of the business':

'The dodgy end of the business has been around for a long time and to some extent the British companies were cushioned by having such a large share of the market. Now we haven't got the strong Commonwealth links, etc., and we're all in there fighting with the rest. I know that in the colleges we have been asked to put on courses on commercial practice for British officers to bring them up to the same standard as the Greeks. They are very good at loading ships in such a way that the ullages [in a tanker, the vertical distance between the surface of the oil and the top of the tank] are favourable to the owners when they're measuring the tanks. If you can, give the ship an imperceptible list to one side, knowing that when the surveyor measure the content of the tank it's going to show up favourably to the company. What you do is simply lean the ship one way when you're loading and the other way at the other end. Or you might load the ship to deliberately hog or sag it. You see, profit margins in bulk shipping at the moment are so fine that if you're not up with all the dodges you're running at a loss.'

In reality, shipmasters were never completely immunised from commercial pressures. But they felt their *effects* and were not involved in making decisions. The function of the master was to deliver the ship, its cargo and its crew safely. There were more pressures, perhaps, on the masters of tramps than on those of liners, because of the ups and downs of trade. Yet masters of all types of ship could find themselves being pressed to make a particular tide or get alongside a berth when weather conditions might suggest less haste and more caution. Stories of transatlantic liners going up Channel with a bone in their teeth in thick fog in order to get alongside on schedule were not without foundation.

The decline of the British fleet has found large numbers of British officers looking for jobs on foreign-flag ships – the officers' union, the Merchant Navy and Airline Officers' Association, reckons that at least 7,000 of its 20,000-plus membership now sail on foreign-flag ships. Many of these ships, although foreign-owned, are operated by British management companies who require high standards of their ships and their crews. Some, on the other hand, are employed on flag-of-convenience ships with unscrupulous owners. A senior union official explained how vulnerable a master might be in those circumstances:

'If the captain has had an accident, perhaps with pollution, then his owner might not be properly covered under the conventions. The ship can be arrested and then the master might be left in a foreign port with no apparent owner and no money to pay the crew's wages, or to feed them, even.

'Perhaps he telephones and says he's got a problem where he suspects water contamination, possible hepatitis and problems of that sort on board where he needs some repairs to be done and the owner just doesn't want to know. He's been told to proceed to the next port, which is the other side of the Atlantic, and is apprehensive of sailing. He asks, what can you do for me? You might wonder what we'd do in that case, but this is where we can use that peculiar relationship which exists between the UK seafarers and the Department of Trade. We can speak to the ship surveyors and say what the problem is and ask, can they alert or pass on through the European ship inspection programme, to say a West German counterpart in Hamburg. Perhaps I'll get a telephone number to ring in Hamburg and ask if one of their surveyors could chance to walk along the quay and go up the gangway to have a look at the crew accommodation and the fresh water situation because the captain's very worried. And so, by 'accident', that ship is stopped and the repairs are done without the owner ever knowing how it came about. It's one way we have of getting at the very bad flag-of-convenience ships.'

For the masters brought up in the post-war traditions of British ships, situations of this sort are almost unthinkable. In all the liner companies, and in most of the tramp companies too, work had more to do with style and technical efficiency. Commerce was something that people in offices did. The general way that seamen had of looking at the world is revealed in Len Holder's remark that 'Of course, you'd get the odd shipmaster with a few shares in the company .... I know I sailed with one, and when we passed another of the company's ships he'd say, "And how did she look?" I'd reply that she looked beautiful, that they'd got the hull and the centrecastle painted ... "I'm not interested in that," he'd say. "Was she down to her bloody marks?" I think if you went on Greek ships of that period the first question would have been "Was she down to her marks?" and the second would be about how little painting you could get away with.'

That is now the order of priority on most British ships, too, but it calls for a turn of mind, for a way of thinking about work that jars and grinds with seafarers who have assimilated a tradition of pride in their ship that was also an expression of pride in self. Most seafarers today, those of them who dare to think and talk about it, are contemptuous of the standards expected to them in maintaining their ships in a regime which Bill Kerrigan describes as 'hurry up and don't stop'. It remains true that the circumstances of their work are extremely demanding. What is true no longer is that the evidence of it is there to be seen, to be remarked upon and be a source of self-congratulation.

[IV] · *Hazard*

The ocean has the conscienceless temper of a savage autocrat spoiled by much adulation ... The most amazing wonder of the deep is its unfathomable cruelty. – *Joseph Conrad*

I

For as long as the statistics have been kept they have told, always, the same tale. Aside from deep-sea fishing, and coal-mining notwithstanding, seafaring is the most dangerous of all occupations. When there are storms around the coasts, then in some newspaper of town or city by the sea there are lines saying that a local seaman has been killed or badly injured. As recently as 1977, when there was still a large British merchant fleet, deaths were averaging 100 per year, owing either to accidents or to casualties to ships. In 1972, after a collision in the river Plate, sixty-four men, the entire crew of the *Royston Grange* were killed. The 80,000 ton bulk carrier *Derbyshire* disappeared without even sending out a distress call when she was caught in a typhoon in the China Sea and took forty-two men with her.

When a ship just disappears with all hands the shock waves take a long time to flatten out, and the *Derbyshire* is a case in point. She has become emblematic of the fears that seamen have of the ocean but rarely express. As Emlyn Williams said, 'Once you stare into the sea you can actually get scared as though the sea wants to draw you in. It's a weird feeling – it looks nice but then you think that it goes down for bloody miles.' The sinking of the *Derbyshire* brought these fears to the surface, and then, of course, in a seafaring community like that of Liverpool there were bound to be large numbers of men who had some connection with the crew.

Joe Gallagher, a motorman on the *Manx Viking*, once spent three years sailing regularly on the same ship down to Brazil with the *Derbyshire*'s engine-room storekeeper: 'You might be thinking about the good times you've had, then all of a sudden you think about him going down in that ship. When I'm on nights down here in the control room I start thinking about it sometimes, and it puts you off.' John Pritchard's fears are less personalised but nonetheless real:

'I was very sad when the *Derbyshire* went down two or three years ago, because my first voyage to sea had been on an older ship of the same name and belonging to the same company. When a ship of that size vanishes off the face of the earth without the slightest bit of a sign it's frightening – and that shows you what kind of weather there is in this world. You know, sometimes people ashore will say to you that they've seen this enormous tanker, and of course some of them really are enormous – but then, to think that they can go down, and not once but many a time.'

The risks that seafarers run are not just those produced by the weather and what it does to the sea. The ship might carry a dangerous cargo, other ships might ignore the rules when navigating in confined waters, you might be visited by pirates off Lagos or in the Malacca Straits who come visiting in canoes powered by large outboard motors. Yet in all these other risks there is something of the human hand, something that seems predictable. The weather and the sea and what it might do to the ship both seem and are random, and so it is this that is feared most. Here, for example, is Dave Kirkwood, who after more than twenty years at sea, first in the Royal Navy and then in merchant ships, does not mind admitting that he is sometimes scared:

'Oh yes, I get frightened. I was frightened last trip when we went through a typhoon. Every time I go up to Japan I get frightened, because that's where the *Derbyshire* went down. We pass over the place very time, and I knew most of the lads in that ship, and I think it could have been me. A typhoon is very frightening when the waves could be anything from fifty to a hundred feet high so that all you can see in front of you is a wall of water – if you can see that far, because sometimes you can hold your hand out and you can't see it because of the spray and rain. In these conditions the ship's being tossed about and you can't do anything about it. All you can do is point your nose into it and let it take you where it wants to. It's not the moving of the ship that frightens you, it's the thought of drowning. I think at the back of every seamen's mind when he goes through bad weather is the thought of drowning. I sometimes have that thought of being in my cabin with the water coming over my head.'

It is difficult to describe how a ship can move in a bad sea, especially if she is in ballast and flying light. Even big ships like the ultra-large tankers of half a million tons can flex and whip like a car aerial. On smaller ships – but large enough by most standards – the middle of the ship might be supported on a wave while the two ends seem to be in suspension. In those conditions, especially if you're amidships, you can actually feel the ship flexing under you. A steel giant is whipping and vibrating. Tony Hinks was aboard a ship that experienced the very same typhoon that sank the *Derbyshire*:

'We were quoted as the nearest ship to it, the *Barber Perseus*, a RO-RO ship. The ship was rolling terribly, but we weren't thinking much of it, because the ship seemed to be going over it. But I remember the cook saying, as he looked aft out of the galley, that he'd never been as frightened, because the deck was sort of twisting, it was snaking and the containers on deck were moving. Eventually we got into Kobe, though we'd had to steam round for a while until the weather abated. I remember coming up off the four to eight and the bosun met me at the top of the lift and he said to me, "Hey, Tony, what ship is your brother on?" I told him that he'd just paid-off the *Derbyshire* and then he told me that she'd sunk. Now that was the only time I've been frightened at sea – but only when I stood back afterwards and thought about it.'

The damage that can be inflicted on a ship in a storm is extraordinary, and here Colum Leggatt describes what happened on his last ship and his reaction to it:

'Last trip we went to Long Beach in California for bunkers and then we set off for Japan. For ten days we got nowhere because of freak storms. It was really frightening, and then at the end of it we found all sorts of cracks and bends in the ship, so we had to put in to Honolulu as a port of refuge. It was a case where your life flashes before your eyes.

'We were fully loaded with four hatches fora'rd and three hatches aft. After this storm we went out and found this crack in the deck. I think everyone lost quite a lot of confidence in the ship after that. I think a lot of us wanted to stay in Honolulu, and certainly I didn't want to go any further ... quite frankly I often find it frightening.

'The trip before last I was in an iron ore carrier and I'd read in *The Telegraph*, the officers' union newspaper, that umpteen of these things have gone out and gone down without a trace. I think this article said it was something like one a month. I think maybe

I've just lost my bottle! I do get frightened at sea, I must admit, and I suppose especially in bad weather; but then you could get half-way across the Pacific and you think that you couldn't get off even if you wanted to.'

On container ships any fears that are induced by the way the ship takes the sea might be compounded by the noises. John Goble says that '... with containers three high on the deck, well, they make a hell of a noise when you're rolling; you know! Empty ones especially are screaching and moaning with a high-pitched tone, they're creaking and groaning with metallic noises. You see, despite the lashings on them they're still getting distorted a bit by the movement of the ship.'

Very few seamen will ever have experienced what they fear most – sailing through the eye of a hurricane. Here Andrew Milligan describes this encounter with the worst that wind and sea can offer:

'Dangerous situations? I went through the eye of a hurricane once, off New Caledonia. That was quite frightening. We'd come out of Brisbane for Panama and anchored for a day in Moreton Bay for repairs and then sailed. The peripheral weather reports passed on through New Zealand had it that the hurricane centre would pass 600 miles ahead of us. Then the reports had it passing astern of us – but none of them ever had us hitting it! But what we found was that the wind was in the same direction all the time. After a few days and about eight o'clock in the morning the sea started building up. By ten o'clock it was blowing like hell. I couldn't tell you what the wind force was – it was off the scale. This continued all afternoon, bloody big waves, and the frequency with which they were hitting the ship really was worrying.

'What frightened me was that we had 1,000 tons of mineral sand in each hatch except No. 5, which was right in front of the accommodation. There was no ballast in this area, so you can imagine the effect it had on the ship. At one end you had all the weight of the cargo and at the other end you had the weight of the engine, so the ship was tending to hog, and there was the fear that she might break her back. The only people who were really worrying about this were the mate and the Old Man and the chief and second engineers, because they were the only ones who knew that the ballast wasn't there.

'The sea had got up by dinner in the evening. We were sitting in the smokeroom playing cards and people were making funny remarks but no one was really laughing. It was very, very dark. It was dark by four o'clock, and it shouldn't have been until half-past six. The sky was overcast. It was pouring with rain and you just couldn't see anything at all. Everybody was a wee bit frightened.

'I went to bed and tried to sleep but couldn't because the ship was rolling and pitching like hell. The frequency of the waves was such that water was just rolling down the foredeck. Before one wave had hit the accommodation another had come over the fo'c'sle head. These big green waves were rolling right down the foredeck, and more or less a solid wall of water was coming right over the accommodation. I'd gone to bed at six – I was second mate then – and at about ten o'clock everything went quiet. I went up to the bridge and the Old Man was there, the third mate, the radio officer and the radio officer's wife. The sky was clear and a thousand birds had landed on the fo'c'sle head, squeaking and screaming.

'There was still a very big swell. A confused swell was rolling and pitching more than I'd seen before. With all that heavy cargo in the bottom of the ship we had a GM of about 11 ft, so the ship was just like a big pendulum. It was deathly silent. The Old Man asked me what I thought we should do. I replied that I thought we should head for the other side of the vortex of the storm as quickly as possible. That took us about half an hour. When we got to the other side the wind started again – we could see the wind blowing the water off the top of the sea. Now the normal thing to do in these circumstances, in the southern hemisphere, is to put your port quarter into it. You adjust your course as you're going out of it so that you always keep it on your port quarter. We did all this, but once again you could see nothing. The water was coming over the stern and just pouring down the front of the bridge. By this time I was on watch, having come on at midnight. The mate was wandering about in his pyjamas wondering what he should do and the Old Man had flaked out on the chartroom settee.

'By half-past seven in the morning the wind had gone down to about Force Seven, which was calm by comparison to what we'd been through. In retrospect, this may not have been a close shave but it was a frightening experience. I'd never been through anything like it before and I never hope to again! What struck me was that even those who didn't known much about the sea knew that something was wrong.

'The birds obviously disappeared when the wind came up again. It was such an eerie thing. There were myriads of birds only on the fo'c'sle head, and you could see them by the light of the masthead light. There were all kinds and there was a hellish noise – a bit like where I live now, where I can sometimes hear the geese from the marsh at night. I suppose they were frightened, though no more than we were, I'm sure!'

After ten years or so at sea, which is time enough to accumulate some experience of a variety of conditions, weather and its effects get taken as part of the job and nobody makes a lot of fuss about them. Ships' masters are especially prone to be matter-of-fact when they talk of bad weather experiences. This is not because they are more modest than other seafarers but because they have learned that that part of their job requires of them a dramatic performance. There are crises that call for a cool nerve, or at least the appearance of one, so that others may also stay cool. Captain Jack Tanner spent most his career at sea trading in relatively small ships from Liverpool and London to Portugal, Spain and other Mediterranean ports. In his last few years at sea he was trading mostly to Portugal: there are a lot of bumpy rides to be had on that run, and the weather off the Portuguese coast can be spectacularly vicious in winter.

'I remember one Valentine's Day. It was the year I finished, and we were off Leixoes. We'd sailed from Lisbon on the 13th and when we got up to Leixoes the weather was so bad we couldn't anchor. There were quite a few ships outside, cruising up and down, and we joined them. Later on that day I was up on the bridge and as the ship went down and then up the foredeck was out of sight because the sea was blown straight along. The wind was that strong – 160 km an hour – the spray was just like a sheet of water. You couldn't see the waves and you couldn't even see the containers that were two high on the deck; you couldn't see the wave troughs and you didn't know when you were going to drop into them. There was a lot of damage done ashore with roads washed away, and in the harbour blocks had been washed off the breakwater into the channel. That was a bad do. Very nasty.

'When we got in the mate said to me that I was the only one that wasn't frightened out there. 'What?' I said. 'I was absolutely petrified!' And I was, too, because you didn't know what was going to happen to the ship because you couldn't see the sea at all, you couldn't judge anything, you couldn't anticipate anything.

Captain Frank Owen, who sailed in the same trade, also has vivid memories of Leixoes:

'I can remember once going into Leixoes in very nasty weather – it was blowing Force Ten and the port was closed. I radioed and told them I was coming in and they told me I couldn't but I went in just the same because we had engine trouble. And then on another occasion I went into the same port in very bad weather and on the way in the ship was lifted bodily sideways. We'd come up from Lisbon, the weather was bad and we were an hour late for the time we were due on the berth. Now in bad weather you usually have a fair idea of when you're taking a chance, and whenever I got to that point I would usually haul off. But on this occasion the agent ashore was going on about how he'd got the gangs of labour waiting for us so that we could sail at midnight, and then you become very conscious of the fact that if you pull off and go and anchor you're losing money for the company ...

'On this particular occasion I told the mate that nobody was to go for'ard and that I'd make my decision as we got up to the breakwater which faces south. Now I was just on the verge of hauling off when the ship was lifted bodily towards the shore, where there are a lot of wrecks. At this point there was no going back, because I couldn't haul off to the west and so I had to go in, because it was the only way I could go! Now that place is always full of fishing vessels, and yet I had to go in at full speed and then come to a grinding halt. That day my legs were literally like jelly.'

For most seafarers, whether in the deep-sea or coastal trades, weather hazards are intermittent. But with the development and recovery of oil and gas from under the North Sea a new branch of the seafaring trade, an extremely dangerous one, has grown up rapidly, mostly manned by refugees from the deep-sea trades who work on ships whose sea movement suggests they were trained in fairgrounds ... Does the job frighten Barry Roberts?

'Yes, it does actually. For me you're talking about a very small ship and in winter very large seas ... it's a case of riding a roller-coaster. The ship is *never* still, it takes horrible rolls and pitches. They're basically submersible at sea. Everything's lashed down and shut in, and you're in what's basically a steel cocoon, because the after deck is usually covered in water because the ship has such a low freeboard, and then you're taking large ones over the bow and they're just running aft.

'There have been times when I thought the windows would come in – especially in a beam sea you see them coming right across at you. Some of those waves are really high and I've been in some terrible rolls where I've thought she wouldn't come back. Some of these seas are vicious, and you can get to the point sometimes where in spite of the lashing down you can feel the cargo start shifting. It just gets to the point where you think that's it, you've had it. There have been times when I've ducked down when I've seen the seas coming at us and thought they were going to get through ... and then you sheepishly get back up and say to yourself that it's really no problem.'

Getting up to the rigs and platforms and then working cargo is something that none of Barry Roberts's previous training in cargo liners running to ports in the Caribbean and the Gulf of Mexico prepared him for. Here in the North Sea he is out on deck working from behind a safety barrier – but like everyone else he wears neither safety harness nor lifejacket. The harness gets in the way of being fast on your feet and the lifejacket makes you too cumbersome to work effectively in loading or discharging cargo:

'The captain drives the ship stern-first up to the rig and then you're sorting out what has to go up and what's coming down and it gets quite hectic at times. It's pretty hazardous. You've got to know what you're doing and be on your toes, especially in marginal weather conditions when it's say Force Six or Seven and the ship is moving quite a lot. We're still handling cargo even when there could be water coming over the back end. You might have a crane that's a hell of a height above you and it's got, say, a container on the end of a long line, and the rise and fall of the ship's stern from peak to trough might be as much as ten feet. When it's that much it's very marginal.'

In the normal course of things in bad weather the people who are up and about in it – the master, mates and ABs – experience the least hazard. They can see the sea-state, the way the ship carries it and moves to it, and can therefore anticipate and calculate the probabilities of what might happen next. And then, unless employed in the North Sea, are not usually engaged in any work that is made appreciably more hazardous by the state of the sea. The watchkeeping mate is on the bridge and doing nothing more dangerous than keeping a look-out, peering into a radar screen and plotting positions off the Decca Navigator if he is anywhere near suitable land.

The more dangerous places to be are in the galley, down below in the engine room or simply moving around in the accommodation. When Frank Owen's ship was lifted bodily towards the shore entering Leixoes, the donkeyman had been coming out of the messroom with a mug of tea, and the movement of the ship threw him into his cabin: 'He'd been thrown about nine to ten feet and had crashed into his desk. On the next roll the other way he was thrown bodily back into the alleyway and then again sent crashing back into his cabin. He was a man in his sixties, a very competent man. He was in tears with the pain and it transpired that he'd fractured his ribs. He was in quite a bad way.'

Even in relatively sheltered waters, like the crossing to Douglas in the Isle of Man from Heysham, the weather can be wicked and totally unpredictable to those below decks. Here Dino Livingstone describes an incident in the winter of 1983 and a characteristic response to it:

'There was one time last winter when a wave hit the side of the ship and I got flung out of my bunk, and when I looked up I saw the horizon lifting up out of my porthole and I thought this was it. I froze with terror, and down in the engine-room control room there's an inclinometer and that went right over. Apparently, down there, there were just pale faces looking at each other and then when she steadied they all started whistling with relief. It is bad at times but you just have to plod on and be stoical, because you don't want to join Maggie's millions, do you?'

The galley is no place to be in bad weather, and it is even worse if the sense of smell has not been immunised by years of wear. Frank Williams is a young second cook and freely admits that ...

'Sometimes I don't feel too good, to be quite honest, when we're in bad weather. It's not that I'm seasick or anything like that, but some of the smells, especially of oil, turn you right off.

The oil in the fryer, lard that's been basted over the joint or spilled in the oven. These are bad smells for me and I don't like them at all. They just turn your stomach over and put you off food, in a way – so I don't eat much food that's cooked in the galley.

'I've only had minor accidents – like a few weeks ago I had a tray of bacon under the grill and there was a lot of oil – bacon fat. The ship took a lurch and the tray shot out. I put my hand out to try and save it and I got this oil over my hand and wrist and it's left me with a scar. A friend of mine, a chief cook, was in bad weather and one of these stockpots went all over him and he's got a big burn scar right down his chest. It really looks bad and he's quite paranoid about it. He was going with some girl and he would never take his T shirt off, never. Now he's going to carry that with him for the rest of his life, and these are the sorts of hazards you've got to put up with.'

Tommy Keefe, who sails as chief cook on the same ship, has the same sort of philosophical attitude. 'It certainly is dangerous – that's why they have pan lids on ships! But you've just got to get on with it, haven't you? I've been on ships where I've actually thought I was going to die. The way the ship went over I thought it was never going to come back. But that's it ... you just get on with it and accept it as part of the job.'

Peter Henderson has been at sea and working in the galley for twenty-five years and graphically describes two incidents in which men might have been seriously injured or even killed:

'The galley is a very dangerous place if you don't know what you're doing. In bad weather you used to have those pan clips on, and even with big pans I've seen those clips go pinging into the air. I had an old bosun with me once who was for ever coming into the gally, and sometimes he used to annoy me if I was busy. Anyway, one time I told him to be careful because I didn't have the clips on the pans and he told me not to worry because he knew what to do. And then, as he walked out of the galley, one of the pans came off after him like it was following him. Another two seconds and he would have been dead, because it was a big pan of boiling scouse.

'My worst experience was on the old *Grecian* one afternoon at four o'clock in really very, very bad weather. You know the way the ship goes over sometimes and she's slow coming back? Well, she took another one, and in those days you used to have a fat pan on the stove. I had a little cook with me called Tommy who weighed about seven-stone-nothing, God rest his soul. The ship took this double lurch and the fat pan started slipping and I was hanging on to a pipe running across the deckhead above me. I was hanging on to this pipe and he was starting to go after the fat pan when he was thrown past me as if he was going downhill. Everything was coming off the stove and I managed to grab hold of him and throw him up on the bench. Everything came off the stove even though it had been lashed on with rope and all sorts. That was the worst experience I've had in my life, because I thought she was going to turn turtle, but at the time I was that concentrated on getting hold of him that I wasn't thinking of the ship.'

Worse even is the engine room, especially if repairs have to be done in a bad sea. An example of how things can be is given here by Tom Calder:

'There was one ship, only about three years ago, on a trip from Galway, on the west coast of Ireland, to Swansea. There's a lot of open sea there and you're out in the Western. We hit bad weather and she was shipping big, heavy seas. The sea was going over the bridge and down the funnel, down vents, down the engine-room skylights. With all of this we got a mass of water into the fuel tanks.

'I was off watch at the time and suddenly everything went black. The engines stopped, and she was really rolling heavily then. We had to get down there and bleed the water out of the system and get the auxiliaries going again and then the main engine. We had a hell of a job, because we'd get it all going for about ten minutes and then more water would come through. All this time the ship was rolling heavily and we were having to hang on with one hand and work with the other. It was a real job just keeping on your feet.

'On that same passage one of the spare cylinder heads broke loose from the bulkhead and smashed one of the valves off one of the air bottles. Then, when we were trying to secure it, it fell down one of the ladders and smashed all the rungs off it. It hit the casing of the main engine, smashed into the flywheel and knocked a couple of teeth off it ... It was on that same trip that we lost one of the life rafts. The seas were that heavy that one came aboard and just tore it off.'

To a very large extent, the way a ship moves in heavy weather depends upon how the weight of her cargo has been distributed in the loading. But no amount of ingenuity by the mate can do very much to amend the way a ship moves if it is, loaded with bulk cargoes like grain, ore, oil, chemicals or gas. But with a general cargo, and perhaps sometimes with containers too, a careful allocation of cargo to different parts of the ship can make a radical difference to the sort of platform provided for the crew. Writing on this topic, Joseph Conrad said:

Ships do want humouring. They want humouring in handling; and if you mean to handle them well, they must have been humoured in the distribution of the weight which you ask them to carry through the good and evil fortune of a passage. Your ship is a tender creature, whose idiosyncrasies must be attended to ...[1]

This is from *The Mirror of the Sea*, which is Captain Fred Patten's favourite Conrad. He read it first when he was a young third mate, and it is tempting to think that he must have taken it to heart, for he says of a class of ships that were notorious for their movement:

'Well, the Hustlers did have a terrific vibration but if you loaded them with a small GM they were quite comfortable. We used to load them with about 800 tons on deck and 1,000 tons below. In very bad weather, other than the worry about the deck cargo moving – and that very rarely happened – they had quite a pleasant motion. Light ship they were unbearable: you couldn't live with them, they were absolute pigs. The GM was absolutely colossal, and so they had an incredibly quick motion. They were designed, you see, to carry very big deck cargoes. In winter time if you had a shortfall on your cargo you put it all on deck and nothing down below at all, because otherwise you couldn't live with them. The motion was so violent you couldn't possibly sleep, you could go for days without sleeping. If they were loaded either deeply or with a good proportion on deck, then they were quite comfortable. The London office didn't like this. They were always thinking there might be a sudden call into another port so that you'd have to shift cargo on deck to get down below, which cost money – but I'm afraid I was rather unsympathetic toward that.'

Those who sailed with Fred Patten and were sufferers from

seasickness were, no doubt, grateful for those occasions when the ship could be loaded to maximise comfort. Seasickness used to be one of those forbidden subjects. It was acceptable to admit to having succumbed on one's first voyage but thereafter a 'proper seaman' was supposed to have got his sea legs and never suffered again. Reality was never that way; today's seafarer is readier to admit to feeling 'off', and some people will confess to being so miserably ill that you wonder at their stamina in going back so regularly for more. There are very few who do not feel a bit queasy when they go back to sea after being on leave, and most adjust after a few days when they have got re-accustomed to the movement, the noise, the vibration, the smells. But the sort of violent movement referred to be Fred Patten and vividly described here by Peter Henderson, who sailed on the same ships, could drive real sufferers to extreme remedies:

'I used to sleep on the deck — I'd take the mattress and put it on the deck and then jam myself in with my life jacket ... One of the skippers on that ship had to nail up his drawers because they were flying out all over the place, and then there was a chief engineer who used to sleep down in the engine room on one of the shelves. In fact he asked me if he could have some linen to take below with him! He used to suffer, did that chief, but then I do myself on the first day out, I feel wishy-washy and can't wait to get to bed. I've even been sick on the Mersey, going down from Garston!'

II

Ships and their crews are most at risk in coastal waters. It is true that ships regularly disappear while on ocean passages, but far more likely is a stranding or a collision when near to land. This being so, it is not surprising that those who spend their days on coastal ships tend to be those with the most experience of sinkings and collisions. Even so, Tom Calder must hold something of a peacetime record for the number of ships of his that have been sunk or badly damaged. The *Normanby Hall* was running from Birkenhead to Belfast with a cargo of flour and animal feed when she ran aground in dense fog. The ship started making water in the holds, the cargo got swollen, blocked the pump suctions and eventually burst open the hatches. At that point everyone got taken off by the Donaghadee lifeboat. Another of his ships, the *Redthorn*, bound from Dunkirk to Antwerp, ran into one of the Townsend Thoreson ferries off Zeebrugge, and when he was on the *Gorsethorn* he had a lucky escape after a collision with a Chinese ship:

'We were on our way down from London to either Calais or Dunkirk and this Chinese ship sheared across and hit us. It hit right at the back of the bridge. Both me and the mate were turned in, both of us off watch at the time. The ship nearly rolled us right over. We could hear the grating and grinding and thought we'd gone ashore. When I tried to get out of my bunk I found I was on the bulkhead, and drawers and all sorts were flying all over the place – my radio went flying past my head. And then when I could look out of my porthole I saw the bow of this ship just sliding off. It had come right to my cabin. Fortunately we were light ship. If we'd been loaded I think we'd have gone down.'

Just four years ago, Tom Calder, at last, really did get sunk by another ship:

'We were going up the Thames in February on the *Blackthorn*. When we anchored off Southend it was dense fog, you just couldn't see a thing. I went up to see the mate to find out what was happening. I was on stand-by down below and I wanted to know whether we'd be going up or not. The mate got word from the pilot station that they'd be sending the pilot out and that we'd be going up. This was a Friday afternoon, so we were well pleased, thinking that we'd have a run ashore that night for a pint, and a sleep-in on Saturday morning.

'We'd been going for a few hours when I felt a slight bump which I thought must be us going alongside the wharf. The next thing, she was starting to go over and a feller at the top of the engine room was shouting at me to get out of her, that she was sinking. When I got up out of the engine room the fog was that dense you just couldn't see a thing.

'The way the ship was we could only launch one lifeboat when the skipper told us to abandon her. We managed to lower the boat and then slid down the deck to get into it. The pilot was in the boat and shining his little torch around and shouting – and we could hear shouting going on all around us. There were ships still moving in the river, in fact one of them nearly ran us down. Then I saw this little red light just above the water and I thought we must have run down a buoy or perhaps hit a wreck. But it wasn't. It was a ship – we'd sunk a ship. It was called the *Frederick K*, a Panamanian ship. It must have sunk like a stone, and the shouts we could hear were the crew in the water. The skipper, mate and engineer of her were British and the rest of the crew were Portuguese. All this happend just off Greenwich. There was nobody hurt or lost on our ship and we got picked up by a tug.

'Standing there on the tug, we were watching our ship lying over. She didn't seem to get any worse, so we went back aboard again. We sounded the tanks and found the forepeak had gone [in the bows of the ship] but the bulkhead was holding. One of the double bottoms had been split right open, the water had rushed in and she'd keeled over. So all we had to do to right her was pump water into the double bottom on the other side. We took her down then to the deep-water berth at Bowater's, and after patching her up berthed at Deptford Creek to discharge cargo and then do more repairs to make her seaworthy enough for a run to dry dock in Hull.'

Jim O'Kane' starkest memory concerns the very same ship but at a time when she was almost new:

'It was in 1961 when we were coming into the Mersey here and bound to Garston. We dropped anchor off Q17 buoy in dense fog and I was the sailor on the watch. The skipper told me to get up on the fo'c'sle head and to ring the bell if I heard any ships blowing. I was up on the fo'c'sle head and I could hear this ship blowing and I was ringing the bell and the skipper was shouting at me to effing well ring the bell louder because there was a ship coming down on us.

'It was the *American Veteran*, one of the United States Line's ships, and from where I was it looked as if he was going to go between our two hatches. I didn't know what to do – whether to jump, run or just hang on to the bell! We were lucky that nobody got hurt or anything, and then, we were light ship. I reckon that if we'd been loaded we'd have gone down. Anyway, the *American Veteran* went on a bit and anchored and the Mersey Radio sent down the Dock Board's salvage ship, the *Vigilant*, to see if we were all right. The cook would have been dead if he'd been in his cabin, because that was wrecked by the collision. She was only a few months old, that ship, at the time – but, my God, that did frighten me!'

The men on the coasters experience double the risks of their deep-sea colleagues. On the one hand they are constantly in the close company of other ships and on the other they experience the same weather hazards as deep-sea men but have those compounded because of their proximity to the land. In the coastal and middle-distance trades to Baltic, Scandinavian and Biscay ports there are some exceedingly nasty bits of water.

The old hands in these trades know all the quiet little anchorages that you can run for when the weather gets out of hand or the passages between the islands on Scotland's west coast that you can take to avoid the worst of wind and sea. But if you are going north about across the top of Scotland, through the Pentland Firth, then there is no shelter. And in this stretch of water even the most experienced are ultra-cautious. One coastal skipper who got his first command when he was twenty-two, and has yet to reach retirement age, said:

'Before I came to this ship I had ten years running from Northern Ireland round the north of Scotland, through the Pentland Firth and down to Blyth. For ten years I was running these ships back and forth. Light ship round, loaded coal in Blyth and then back again. Sometimes up there it's not just a gale, it's a hurricane. That's quite regular up there, and you get that way that you're always listening to forecasts, all the time. You have to be very careful up there. Even for us who are well used to it, going through the Pentland Firth can be like going through the gates of hell.

'Sometimes you might have a hurricane of wind behind you. Now that type of situation is difficult, because you can't turn her round and go back and there's nowhere you can dodge into and anchor. Sometimes it's a good job it's dark and you can't see what's happening! Now, of course, going back with a cargo of coal in you it's not so bad. In the winter time the ship's decks are full of water all the time when she's loaded but there's no use worrying about it. That's just part of the job.'

Captain Mike Johns, who served his apprenticeship with one of the great liner companies, and who had his first job as a young officer on one of those grand lilac-hulled Union Castle ships that used to run down to South Africa, has spent the last few years on coasters and middle traders. And he does not mind confessing that he finds coasting produces far more anxiety than trading deep-sea: 'Going north about, through the Pentland Firth, is something new for me. I was terrified at first and just couldn't imagine doing it light ship. But these chaps on these ships think nothing of it. For someone who hasn't done it for years and years like these people it really is a bit frightening at first.'

Jim O'Kane is one of those experienced people who have been through the Pentland Firth many times in the last twenty-five years, and although he seems to take it all for granted there is a respectful wariness when he talks about the power of the sea. In mid-October 1983 the whole of Britain experienced Force Ten winds ... and Jim O'Kane was on passage from Teesport to Ghent, in Belgium. 'The whole ship was awash, the boat deck and all. We were taking them green over the whole ship, and it's then that you say what the hell are you doing with a job like this. Is this what you have to do to earn a shilling?' And this reminds him then of 'going north about':

'On a ship like this and in bad weather a trip that ought to take a day might take two or three days. In winter I've known it take a week to get from Northern Ireland to Blyth light ship. There, you'd be working your way round the coast from one anchorage to another. This was normally a two-day run, but it took us from a Saturday to the following Saturday to get from Londonderry to Blyth. We left in the afternoon and made a passage up the west coast of Scotland and got across the north of Scotland as far as Donnet Bay – that's near Thurso – and we were at anchor in there for about a day and a half and then we managed to get down into the Moray Firth and lay there for a day. Then the weather started to moderate, so we made a passage as far down as the Longstone, off the Farne Islands, only thirty-five miles from Blyth. But then the weather turned again and we had to turn back and anchor off Leith for the rest of the week. Finally we left Leith early on the Saturday morning and got down to Blyth the same afternoon.'

On some passages, however, there is nowhere to hide and you might have a cargo in your ship that seems designed to make life a torment. In the winter of 1983 Mike Johns was master of a ship called the *Camilla Weston*, running between the Baltic and the UK. 'I was telling a colleague of mine about this, and he said he wouldn't want to do that. That on a small ship like that one you could easily get lost crossing the North Sea in winter. In fact on one occasion we were taking feed-wheat pellets from Leith and coming back with steel plate, and he reckoned I had to be mad taking cargoes like that in such a small ship on that run in winter. You see, with a cargo like that all the weight is in the bottom of the ship and the rolling motion is terrible. Coming across there, there's nowhere to run to, and in fact I did come across in a Force Ten last winter.'

Glen Broughton is another former deep-sea seafarer now working in the coastal and middle trades, and he recalls a heavy-weather trip across the Bay of Biscay in November 1982:

'I was in one of Hadley's, a fifteen-ninety-niner, one of those designed to keep just outside the regulations which make you carry a radio operator and so on. We were off Cape Finisterre, running china clay from Fowey to Gaeta, which is just north of Naples in Italy. The weather was really bad and the seas following us were madness. It was that bad that we had to heave to, which meant coming round, taking the weather on the beam before we could get her head up into the weather.

'In our vicinity there was a Spanish ship that was sinking, a small gas carrier. The crew had abandoned ship and then Spanish Air Force planes came and bombed the ship, blew it out of the water because of the hazard to other ships. We didn't see any of this but we could hear the reports coming in over the radio.

'For ourselves, we just seemed to time things nicely and round head to the weather. The swell was mountainous – it was above the funnel, for God's sake! One minute it was towering over you and the next minute you were looking down into it. I can tell you, it was really scary! While we were turning into the sea I don't mind telling you my heart was going a bit and there were several moments when I thought we were going to cop it.'

Coming up or down Channel, whether it is from Ushant one way and inward bound or from Hamburg the other way and outward bound, all the traffic is inevitably funnelled through the bottleneck at the Straits of Dover. Most ships are routed into inward and outward lanes and are continuously informed by radio of any hazards, wayward ships and the giant tankers and bulkers which draw so much water that in certain places they cannot easily alter course to take avoiding action. For the inexperienced young mate it has all the apparent chaos that once marked Piccadilly Circus on a Saturday night: there are the lights of other ships everywhere, and sometimes it can seem as if they are coming down at you, line abreast, across from the English to the French shore. And if you look at the radar screen with untutored eyes chaos seems worse compounded, for it is covered with the orange blip echoes of a thousand fireflies. The practice of sailing through this seething crowd, however, is not so nightmarish. In fact Noel Pereira, who passes through the Channel fairly regularly in 200,000 tonners on his way to Rotterdam's Europort, says:

'It's a piece of cake. Because of the traffic separation zones there's no problem. Everybody is going the same way, apart from the odd rogue ship. Generally the lane discipline is excellent and all you have to do is identify the ship up ahead of you ... Now when it comes to crossing traffic I don't bother. I don't bother about ferries, I just keep going. With the ferry people you cause more chaos if you start manoeuvring. I'm talking about being on a ship with a restricted draught. Often it's not a question of sea room but of draught. What I'll often do if I see a ferry coming to across ahead, I'll call him up on the radio if I can read his name through the glasses and tell him what my course and speed are. And what I find is that they'll tell me to stay on course and say they'll clear me by half a mile.'

Perhaps his optimism is similar to that of the juggernaut driver who is so confident of his intimidating size that he can be fairly certain that no one is going to argue with him. Certainly the view from the ferries is somewhat different. In the story that follows the officer telling it understandably preferred to be anonymous:

'Whilst I was working in a ferry company we were going up from Dover to Zeebrugge, and the last part of that's in a buoyed channel. I was up on watch, and it was normal practice to keep to the starboard side of the channel, and on those ships the captain doesn't generally come up until you're a mile off the breakwater.

'There was this ship coming down the channel from Antwerp and there's this sort of bend in the channel where the traffic from that direction would alter to starboard and you'd pass port to port – but for some reason he held on longer than was normal at night. I think then I just froze and sort of murmured something to the helmsman about going to port, and the next thing this feller just whizzed down our starboard side and I don't really know why or how we missed him. I just sort of stood there ... I didn't really do anything ... I just froze, really.

'Then the captain came up after I'd rung him and I told him that I'd just had this altercation with a bulk carrier who was sticking to the middle of the channel – and he asked me why I hadn't gone outside the buoy! And then I said to him that I didn't know that one! Although I'd done about thirty runs by then, I'd never had a situation like this one, and of course to go outside the buoys is a big taboo to us deep-sea men.

'How did we miss him? I don't know. But almost certainly because of the action of the other ship, because I certainly didn't do anything positive. I wasn't in control of the situation at all.'

A shipmaster's worst fear is of an engine failure when making port or close to the land. It is for that reason that deep-sea masters often appear to be afraid of the land and, when on an ocean passage that requires skirting a headland or a run along a coast, give instructions to the mates to pass a good distance off. Indeed, for the second mate, who lays out the courses on the charts for each leg of the voyage, it will be routine for him to ask the master how distant he wants to pass those pieces of land that mark turning points.

Engines, nevertheless, cannot always be relied upon to fail at convenient moments, as Fred Patten once found. 'The worst fright I had in recent years was when we were leaving Beirut and the bedplate of the main engine cracked; the engine seized and we were totally immobilised. It was during the troubles ashore as well, and there was a curfew, so the whole port was closed down at night. This happened just before the curfew, and we just drifted down the coast. Fortunately the weather wasn't too bad, because there was no hope whatever of fixing the job. The engine was a complete write-off at the time, because it took about three months in dry dock to put it right.

'There was an old tug in Beirut, just one old tug. Luckily I managed to get hold of this chap who was the head pilot and whom I'd known for years, and his son brought this tug out. By this time we were only a quarter of a mile off the rocks, but in deep water. You've got deep water there right up to the beach, almost. So we managed to get back – but only just.'

III

There are few engineers who have not had to cope with an engine-room fire at some time in their career. The typical fire will have been small and quickly got under control. Those who work down in the confined machinery spaces where oil is everywhere know well how vulnerable they are and do not waste any time when the threat appears. And yet so everyday is the possibility that stories about fires tend to be delivered in the same matter-of-fact way as stories from other members of the crew about flying fat in the galley or white water in the Pentland Firth. Here Dario Vieceli talks about one of his nastier experiences:

'Another tight corner I was in was when we had a fire while we were in the Mersey. The ship had just come out of dry dock and they had fitted a whole load of new fuel cocks. Because of a defect I had shut off the fuel leading to the main engine, and then one of the fuel cocks blew off, and so a fine spray of fuel oil was going all over the engine room. Things were already starting to run red-hot and I shouted 'Stop the engine, stop the engine', but with this fuel oil going everywhere the engine room just burst into flame. I was covered myself, and how I didn't get burned I don't know. We grabbed the fire extinguishers and tried to put the fire out but it wasn't much use.

'We couldn't see each other. The third was standing right next to me, but I could only feel him, and the chief was only three or four feet away but I had no idea where he was. We decided to get out of the engine room, hoping that the chief had gone, because I couldn't find him. I'd been in the ship some time and knew my way around by feel, but the third had just joined and I thought he was right behind me. In fact he'd missed his way and was lucky to find his way out by another route.

'When I got out I found the chief wasn't there, so I ran up to the bridge because I knew he'd phoned the bridge to say we were on fire. When I got to the bridge I told the captain we were on fire and that the chief was trapped below. The captain said that seeing as we were in the channel there was nothing he could do. This captain was one of these slow-thinking, pipe-puffing types, so I said to him, well, at least sound the alarms – all this was going on at one in the morning. It didn't seem to occur to him that if we were on fire we weren't going to be going anywhere anyway!

'Anyway, he sounded the general alarm and I ran back to the bottom alleyway and found the chief had got out. It was his first trip back after a cartilege operation and I was thinking that he was killed on his first trip back. Eventually we got the fire under control and then we had to be towed back in. We got everything temporarily right again after two days. Down below everything was black, it was just like being up a chimney ... and then we had this damned director who knew nothing whatever about ships wanting to know why we hadn't continued with the voyage, since the damage was relatively slight!

'I'd been in a fire before, in a Larrinaga ship, but in those big engine rooms there was room to move and see what was happening. But this was really frightening because in these small engine rooms once you go on fire it spreads that fast that within seconds you can't control it. Once we were on deck and had battened everything down I was beginnning to think we might have to abandon ship, and the thought of that really frightened me. So having gone through all this I was pretty angry at what this director had said. All he was thinking about was saving a day when thirteen or fourteen men could have been killed.'

Potentially far more lethal than engine-room fires are some of the cargoes carried in the gas and chemical tankers which regularly use rivers and estuaries passing through densely populated conurbations. John Pritchard describes one of these ships which sails regularly down the Manchester Ship Canal from Runcorn, into the Mersey and then across the Irish Sea to Northern Ireland:

'With that ship there is no room for error. If that ship had a major accident it would just vent off all its chlorine, which would form a gas cloud which would then drop off over Liverpool if the wind was from the south-west and goodness knows how many people would be at risk. That stuff paralyses your lungs and on that ship, the *Pole Star*, everyone has a breathing apparatus in the wardrobe in their cabin, and we have that on the chemical carriers too. Then the wheelhouse, which is the part of the ship designated as an evacuation area, has twelve BA [breathing apparatus] sets and the wheelhouse is hermetically sealed so that you can operate from inside there in the event of anything happening to the ship.

'It's deadly. The traffic controllers are on red alert when that ship comes down the river, and she comes down seven times a

month. They're all deadly, all these chemicals, but you just do
your job. You just get on with it as if you were carrying a cargo
of water. I've never sailed on the *Pole Star*, though I've been
abroad just to look around. She's only small but she's a lethal
little job.'

John Pritchard usually sailed on ships carrying acrylo-nitrile,
a chemical that among other uses goes into acrylic artificial
wools. Matt Bainbridge sailed as bosun in these ships, which
trade mainly between the various chemical plants on each side
of the North Sea. Of acrylo-nitrile cargoes he says:

'When I was first on ships carrying it they claimed there was
no great danger from it. It has a very pungent smell, like bitter
almonds, and it's also a water-finding thing. It heads for your
eyes, your mouth, for anywhere that's wet. If you're down below
and you haven't got your sea boots on, it goes up your trouser leg,
and if you're sweating a bit around the crutch – well ...! At first
it was reckoned to be unpleasant but relatively harmless. Now
they've found that it's a carcinogen. The safety level threshold,
in my opinion, is pretty dubious, because they keep on adjusting
it. With this acrylo-nitrile, for example, they've changed the level
from twenty parts in a million to two in a million.'

Safety procedures on these ships are normally rigorous and
closely observed. But within the ship's crew the weight of respon-
sibilities in the running of the vessel falls unevenly, and this in
turn inevitably affects how safety procedures are in practice
operated. The master and mate may be responsible for the safety
of the crew but they are also under constant pressure from the
ship's operators to deliver and collect cargoes promptly. In these
circumstances, and despite what rules may specify, there is a
point at which the obligations to owners and to crew begin to
separate. Ratings and petty officers are not affected by these
conflicting loyalties and interests in the same way, and that is
why the safest ship is one where there is someone like Matt
Bainbridge to take a close and articulate interest in safety
questions:

'Where I'm concerned we do things by the book, and, generally
speaking, everybody else goes along with that. I know on some
ships the mates push it a bit because they're in a hurry, and I've
even seen some of the crew say that we seemed to go to a lot of
trouble. One of the ABs said to me that on his previous ship

the bosun would say things like 'This sorts out the men from the boys', and would go down a tank without testing it first. I'm not saying that the 'macho' thing is general, but it is there. It's so stupid, but it's very difficult to stop it.'

Feeling themselves to be the successors to the allegedly hard-case men of the sailing ships, ABs and male deck cadets are the most prone to risk-taking as a means of proving themselves proper men and true seafarers. On the other hand, and especially on the gas and chemical carriers, accidents find crew members without anyone looking for them. Dave Kirkwood explains what can be expected from a cargo of ammonia:

'The worst thing I've encountered since I've been on these gas ships was when we were carrying ammonia and there were three of us putting a new runner on the derrick. The derrick was down over the manifold, and one morning as we were steaming along the mate, as usual, vented off the gas. It must have got into a down-draught eddy, because I got the full brunt of it. I couldn't breathe. I just stopped, and I felt myself going over. Fortunately my mate saw what was happening, caught me and threw me over on to the deck. When I came out of it about ten minutes later I was burnt all under my arms. The ammonia had got to the soft parts of my body where I was sweating, and I was red raw.

'I've had a few blasts of it since, but never as bad as that. The majority of fellers working on these ammonia ships are going to get a whiff sooner or later. It's there all the time, you see – the smell of it's always there. We often talk amongst ourselves about whether there might be some long-term effects.

'When you're carrying ammonia then during the normal working day you must carry a respirator all the time. Ammonia eats metal, it's very hungry stuff, so there are always little leaks here and there, and you can't see it. You could be just walking along and all of a sudden you'll get some of it and it stops you breathing immediately and then you put your respirator on quick.'

Of course, dangerous chemicals were carried on ships long before the arrival of specialist bulk carriers, and Jack Tanner has a vivid recollection of how nearly every member of his crew was affected by leaking drums in the cargo:

'On one trip on the *Aegean* we went first to Marseilles and then on to Genoa. After we'd left Marseilles the crew started to

complain about colds and so I thought it was a bug going round
the ship. We had a crew of thirty-nine, and thirty-three wanted
to see the doctor − they had pains in their chests and sore throats.
As soon as I'd cleared the ship into Genoa I asked for a doctor
and this Polish chap came down. He examined the crew and
said, along with me, that he thought it was a virus.

'The next day they were still moaning and groaning, and
that evening I went to see the steward in his room. While I was
in there the mate came in, and he took me up to No. 3 hatch,
on the boat deck. The stevedores had lifted out drums of cargo
which were for Leghorn and had been put to one side so that the
Genoa cargo could be got at. The mate pointed to one drum
which had a big skull-and-crossbones painted on it, and it was
sinking into the deck: it was burning a hole. I took one look
at this and its warnings, which included "Do Not Inhale" ...
Luckily we had a 'phone aboard the ship, and I asked the doctor
to come down right away and I showed him the drum. We looked
through the manifest and we identified the manufacturer, but
it only had a trade name, so it didn't mean anything to the
doctor.

'I went down to the 'phone again and rang Liverpool. It was
the general manager who answered. I told him what the problem
was and asked him to find out what was the antidote. Then we
waited for about an hour until he 'phoned back to say that he'd
been on to the makers and they were sending out two doctors and
a decontamination squad and they'd be arriving at four in the
morning. They'd chartered a plane and put them all in it.

'Now that same morning the steward had woken me at about
four o'clock to ask me to go and look at the second engineer. He
had a handkerchief to his face, which was red with blood, and his
pyjamas were red too and he was coughing ... I called for the port
doctor and then an ambulance came in no time and whisked him
off to hospital. At that time we thought this was an advanced case
of TB ...

'When I heard that this decontamination squad was on its way
I was an absolute nervous wreck. When the Polish doctor came
to my room he could see the state I was in and asked me if I had
a bottle of whisky. I said I had, thinking he wanted to take a bottle
with him, and by that time I would have given him anything.
Anyway, he took the top off, crushed it in his hand and threw it

away. Then he got two glasses and said we were going to drink the bottle, because I needed it!'

Jack Tanner was fortunate in being in port and in being able to get specialist help quickly. Ships at sea on ocean passages, unless carrying passengers, will carry neither a doctor nor any crew member with any medical training beyond rudimentary first aid. As a consequence the well-being of a crew member who becomes seriously ill quickly becomes an international emergency and the radio oficer a key link in summoning aid. Howard Benson relates the part he played in getting medical attention for one of the engineers on a tanker off West Africa and bound for Cape Town:

'The captain, unable to find any satisfaction from the *Shipmaster's Medical Guide*, the standard work carried on British ships, had instructed me to send out an XXX MEDICO for a ship carrying a doctor, as our sick engineer was becoming worse and his temperature was rising dangerously. XXX is the next in priority to SOS, the distress signal, and it was with some sense of occasion that I transmitted the immortal letters, followed by our position, and sat back to await results. As anticipated, a doctor at sea is a rare creature indeed, and there was no doctor forthcoming. Equally predicatable, though, was the welcome call from a Russian fish factory ship which carried a para-medic, as do so many Russian vessels. After some three or four hours during which the Russian radio officer and myself exchanged signals, using the international Q codes, and obtained radio bearings on one another's ships using Radio Direction Finder, we rendezvoused in a typical West African coastal mist and lay half a mile off one another to await VHF contact between the respective captains.

'To complete the story, the Russian medic came over without mishap on a smooth, oily sea – again typical of the equatorial region – and duly ministered to the sick man, who recovered after a few days of Russian medicaments. It is a sad reflection on Western countries that so often when medical assistance is required from another vessel it is a Russian para-medic who comes to our aid. Why don't we train men to this standard?'

Deaths, and then burals, at sea are nowadays rather rare. It seems appropriate, nevertheless, to end a chapter on hazard with an account of the burial of a Somali seamen who died while on a sulphur carrier and during a transatlantic voyage. John Goble was the mate:

'This was the first burial at sea I'd been involved in, thank God. We had a problem to find something to put him in – this was a tanker. The Old Man said that in the old days we used fire-bars but the chief said that he couldn't help there, since this was a motor ship! And then I had to say that we hadn't any canvas.

'In the end we used a big PVC cover off the insurance wire reel. Fortunately I had a very good deck mechanic on board, a Portuguese from the Cape Verdes, and he made a beautiful job of stitching him up. And then the bosun found an SWL 25 ton (Safe Working Load) shackle, the sort of thing you'd *never* normally find on a tanker, and that was put in the bag with the Old Somali as a weight.

'Now Denholm's, as you might expect, was not a great firm for uniforms, but the Old Man thought we should put on our uniforms as a mark of respect. We assembled on the weather deck when we were just somewhere north-east of Bermuda. The weather was pleasant and the ship had just a bit of a roll. At the appointed time we slowed down and then stopped engines and gathered round right next to one of these great big mushroom vents from one of the sulphur tanks. Now every time the ship rolls the sulphur is swilling around down there and then the gases come up, force a flap open in the vent and send out a great cloud with a noise like somebody forcing out a breath. We got covered with a yellow dust, because the gas had sulphur in suspension.

'Well, the Old Man read the standard burial service and then the head man from the engine room wanted to say some verses from the Koran. You see, we asked him if he wanted a Christian burial and he told us that that was what he wanted, because he liked to see a man get a good send-off, but that afterwards he'd like to read a bit from the Koran. This went on for about twenty minutes, and there we were, getting covered in sulphur in our best uniforms and with tears in our eyes. He certainly got a good send-off!'

[V] · *Voyages*

Landfall and departure mark the rhythmical swing of a seaman's life and of a ship's career. – *Joseph Conrad*

I

The final disappearance of the coal-burning ship apart, little else of any substance had markedly changed in the life of the seafarer in the twenty three years which elapsed between George Hardy's first voyage in 1944 and his first command in 1967. His first trip as master took him to Java and Malaysia on what was a thoroughly familiar routine for a Blue Funnel ship. 'The outward cargo was manufactured everything-you-could-think-of. Homeward it would be copra, timber, spices, pepper. There was palm oil and latex, mainly from Sumatra, and then there was tin and rubber from Malaya.'

Only five years before, the very same ship had been a regular caller at the beach ports in the island archipelagoes of South East Asia. 'Up in the Sangi Islands and around the Celebes and then between the Celebes and the Philippines you'd just steam in with so many shackles out on your anchor and when it caught the bottom you were there! You had these small three-ton tugs on deck with their barges. You'd pick these up in Macassar and then take them round the out-ports. Of course we only loaded in these places and it was mainly copra, unless you went to the Borneo coast and up the rivers, in which case it was logs which had been floated down.'

George Hardy's last command was far, far distant from anything with such a flavour of Conrad. It was a 64,000 ton container ship which ran like a seaborne goods train from European ports to the Far East:

'The round voyage is two months, and most of that is sea time. Let's start the voyage from Hamburg. We get twenty-four hours in Hamburg, and that's a long time. We'll get, say, eight hours in Bremerhaven, possibly twenty-four hours in Rotterdam, eight hours in Le Havre and twenty-four in Southampton. We'll do a crew change and take stores in Southampton and we'll have taken bunkers in Rotterdam. Then it's out through the Suez and first stop is Port Klang in Malaysia, where we'll maybe get eight hours. Then it'll be eight hours in Singapore and twelve in Hong Kong. Then it's perhaps twenty-four hours in Kaohsiung – that's in Taiwan – and this is the turnaround port.

'If you're going to Japan then you're going all the way from Suez to, say, Tokyo in about twenty-one days at twenty-one knots. There are about nineteen ships on the service and it can get a bit like a shunting yard – if one ship gets delayed, then it goes clang-clang-clang down the line. As a result, the speed might get varied on passage so that the ships don't pile up as it were.'

Identical ships run the Australasian service with an identically breathless service, although there is rather more chance of perhaps a couple of nights in Melbourne or Wellington. Even so, it is still a two-and-a-half-month round voyage and does not even approximate to what used to be the leisurely life on a cargo liner with as much as eight weeks round the New Zealand coast. Until the mid-1960s there were as many as fifty ships engaged at any one time on New Zealand voyages to and from the UK. All that now remains of this are fewer than ten ships taking frozen lamb from New Zealand to Persian Gulf ports. Their crews count themselves lucky to get a total of two weeks ashore.

So rapid and so relatively recent have been the changes in types of ship, port stay and voyage pattern that most seamen over the age of twenty-five have had experience of what can now only be referred to as a 'traditional' way of life. And the older the seafarers the more grounded in those traditions are their conceptions of what it means to be a 'proper seafarer'.

Especially for those who are over thirty there is bound to be a profound contrast between their present and their past. We have already seen something of this in the beginning and end points of George Hardy's career. Here, in a segment of Captain Jack Woods's life history, the divergence is even more striking. Jack Woods is now master of the *Manx Viking*, a Sealink ferry on the run between Heysham and Douglas in the Isle of Man. The ship runs to a timetable which varies only in really foul weather. In the winter months every night is spent alongside the quay in Douglas, and for those who live in the Isle of Man it is almost like a shore job. This style of seafaring could not be more different for Jack Woods than his first experiences. He joined his first ship when he was sixteen years old, in 1957. He got home again, for just five days, three years later. Apprenticed to a P & O subsidiary which operated a fleet of ships permanently based in India, he spent his first two years on a ship which loaded coal in Calcutta for Rangoon, rice in Rangoon for Colombo, where, after two months discharging, the ship returned to Calcutta for more coal for Rangoon and then took more rice to Colombo ...

'Colombo was notorious for its delays. It hadn't a port big enough to cope with the volume of traffic, so you had to wait. Sometimes you had to anchor out, but mostly they'd take you on to the buoys in the centre of the harbour. What would happen was that you'd spend three or four weeks doing nothing and then a gang would arrive and discharge a couple of hundred tons and then you wouldn't see them again for another two or three weeks. Thinking back, it was almost as if we were waiting for the people to eat the rice!

'When we finished it was light ship up to Calcutta and then load coal. It was all loaded by hand – 8,000 tons of it in about eighteen hours! It was like an endless stream of ants – the coolies with the little baskets on their heads. There's be a big mountain of coal on the quayside. Now the ship was level with the quay and they'd put the hatchboards between the ship's deck and the quay to form gangways and there'd be two of these for each hatch – one 'on' and one 'off' – and we had five hatches. There'd be women, children and men – whole families – and literally thousands of people altogether, and they each had sort of large fruit baskets and they'd go to the pile of coal and some feller would shovel it in and then they'd put the basket on their head, walk up to the hatch, dump it over and go back to join the queue for another load. They used to get paid so much a basket, and so every time they went past the tally clerks they'd be given a straw and at the end of the day they'd be paid accordingly.'

Jack Woods came home when his indentures expired. He was twenty. After six months' leave he was on his way as a passenger, on the *Queen Elizabeth*, to New York to join a Booth Line ship, the *Verras*. Based in New York, the ship ran down through the Caribbean chain of islands and then up the Amazon and back to New York in a three-month round trip. After doing four or five of these you went home for some leave. Jack Woods kept this routine for five years:

'Out of New York the first port was Antigua, where we'd arrive in the morning and sail in the evening and then we'd do St Kitt's, Martinique, Guadaloupe, Dominica, Grenada, Barbados, Trinidad. We only had small parcels for each: food, whisky, cigaretes, the odd car – American Hands across the Sea and that sort of thing. By the time you got to Trinidad you'd more or less discharged all your cargo except perhaps a little bit for Brazil. Then we'd go up to Venezuela and load about a thousand tons of cement and off we chugged then, down to Brazil, to the Amazon. We'd touch on Belem, which is about a hundred miles up river from the sea, and then to Manaos.

'Manaos is about 800 miles from the sea and that would take us about five days. From Manaos to Iquitos was about another 1,200 miles and would take us about seven days. Coming down, we'd do it in about two days, because there are tremendous currents. You've got about 2,000 miles of navigable river, and I think there were then about two buoys and one lighthouse on it!

'We had Brazilian pilots taking us up to Manaos and Peruvian pilots from there up to Iquitos. You'd be going all the time, night and day. The pilot's criterion was that if he could see both banks of the river they would go, and if they lost one of the banks they would anchor. Now you can imagine what it would be like with no radar and some pretty heavy rain. It wasn't so bad going up, because you were stemming the tide and it was easy to ease back and drop anchor, but coming down you would be hurtling along at eighteen knots and suddenly the heavens would open and you couldn't see a damn thing. Then the pilot would be ordering hard a-port and you were letting go the anchor and crashing into trees and branches and God knows what.

'There was plenty of water up there, although low river was a bit difficult because then there was a lot of shoaling. It wasn't a surveyed river – it was pure local knowledge of the pilots, and I must say that they were very, very good. They knew where the position of the channel was likely to change, and so sometimes the pilot would order 'stop', drop the anchor and then go off in a little speedboat we carried which was equipped with a transistorised echo-sounder to find the channel. The pilot would be sitting there looking at the sounding machine and giving instructions to go this way and that and at the same time he'd be looking at trees and points to give himself some leading marks. He'd get all this in his head and never write anything down, and then we'd go back to the ship and start off again. Those Peruvian pilots were amazing people.

'Logs floating in the river were the biggest problem at night – monstrous great Amazon trees, rain-forest trees. Most of these would be semi-submerged or even completely submerged. Going up at night you might hear this great clonk as you hit a log, so you really had to be standing by the telegraph all the time so that you could ring the engines to stop and hope the prop. would stop turning before it hit a log.

'We'd get up to Iquitos with about a thousand tons of cement, though I'm not sure what they did with it – we used to reckon they used it as flour to make bread with! Iquitos is just a little clearing in the jungle. It's got just one concrete road and the rest is mud track. We'd be there for a week. It was a very quiet town but the people were very friendly and ours were the only ships that ever went there. There was never any trouble, and we used to get taken out to barbecues and parties. For entertainment it was one of the best ports we went to. It wasn't like Hell-fire Corner down Rio way or anything like that – it was rather civil-ised. Because you were a regular visitor and few ships went there you sort of got accepted into the community. It wasn't one of those ports where you're *just a seaman*. They'd be down in their cars to see you come alongside and they'd come down to see you off. It was a bit like being part of the family.'

Jack Haywood is a fifty-two-year old carpenter/AB who also spent some years with Booth Line, though his ships were on the Liverpool to Manaos service, and on these some of the crew were petty traders in Brazilian livestock. 'In some part there might be a lot of parrots, and a couple of the lads were really into that. Then there were those small monkeys – marmosets – and then sometimes a snake might get into the cargo. Some of the ABs were getting monkeys and parrots to bring home – anything they could make a few bob on. All they needed was a licence from the Ministry of Agriculture to import the parrots. On this one ship I've seen as many as thirty parrots, and the company started charging freight at $30 a bird!'

This was in the early 1960s when a sailor might still bring back, *almost* literally, a parrot on his shoulder or a canary from the Canaries. But in more recent years Jack Haywood has twice been made redundant from what were once regarded as impregnable liner companies. Now his life is a sort of deep-sea equivalent of running across the Irish Sea. A year or so ago he got sent out to South Korea to join a gas carrier:

'She was on charter to some Korean outfit and we just laid in this place called Yosu as a storage ship. An LPG [liquid propane gas] terminal was being built ashore but wasn't finished, so we just lay there for storage. A ship would come and fill us with LPG and then we'd distribute that to little coasters that went round the Korean coast. That was really tedious.

'Now I'm about to join this ship, the *Devonshire*, in Suez. We're flying out and I'm going to replace a feller who's just killed himself, so that's a good sign! I don't like the job as much as I used to. You see, these ships are tramping and you never know where you're going. All I know is that from Suez we're going to the States, but we could go anywhere after that, and I'll be on it for a minimum of four months and a maximum of five. But it's a job and it pays the rates!'

Tramping was what most oil tankers did in the past and many still do today. All that has changed is the confidence the crew may usually have about the duration of their stay aboard ship. In the mid-1960s, however, and as Andrew Milligan discovered, *nothing* was predictable about tanker life, least of all in ships on charter to an oil company. Looking for a job as third mate to see him through the summer months until the nautical college opened again in the autumn, he was sent to the 20,000 ton *Thirlby*, owned by Ropner's of West Hartlepool and lying in the Queen Elizabeth II oil dock at the entrance to the Manchester Ship Canal:

'The *Thirlby* hadn't been off the European coast for nine months, and after I joined we went round to the east coast and did a few ports there and went across to Rotterdam and Antwerp ... Twenty days had passed, and we were in Santander. We had finished discharging and we were supposed to go back to Thameshaven.

'We sailed from Santander at about one o'clock in the afternoon, and when I came down off the bridge I went below, wrote my notice for the Old Man and got the chief steward to witness it so that I could get paid off in Thameshaven. After that I lay down for the afternoon and, come five o'clock, went up to relieve the mate for his tea.

'When I went up to the bridge I thought the sun was in a funny place. The sun was right ahead of us, and I thought: this wasn't quite right, it should have been on the port side ... "There's your course, 270," the mate said, and then told me what traffic there was about and where it was heading. I said, "Thank you very much," and went to look at the chart to find the course laid off for Finisterre and from there it went off into mid-Atlantic. I came back six months later!

'From Santander we went to Aruba in the Dutch West Indies and from there to Trinidad to load again for Lagos and Dakar. When we got to Lagos it was just in time to experience the Biafrans bombing Lagos harbour. We were carrying aviation spirit, too, so it was very pleasant for us on this tanker!

'After that we went back to the Caribbean, did several trips up and down to New York, went up the west coast of the States as far as Seattle and at one time we were heading down for San Francisco or thereabouts, possibly to load for Vietnam, and I was thinking that I just couldn't take this. All sorts of ideas of jumping ship went through my head at the time, but in the end we didn't go to Vietnam and we came home a few weeks later after being away for six months.'

Fifteen years later, in 1978, Elizabeth Flynn joined a tanker as a deck cadet in different circumstances. She was flown out to Cape Town and then helicoptered out to the 270,000 ton ship which was on its way to Kharg Island in the Persian Gulf. Four and a half months later she left the ship in Cape Town to be flown home for leave. Her next two voyages were typical for a tramping tanker:

'I joined in Melbourne this time, and the ship was trading around Papua New Guinea, Fiji and Australia. We got strike-bound on this ship in Australia. It was Christmas Eve and we had Christmas in port near Melbourne. From there we sailed to Bangkok and then to Singapore to load for Japan. Then it was back to Singapore and then on to Aden. Then we went to Kandla, which is up the Gujerat in the Gulf of Kutch. I paid off in Kandla. It's in the middle of nowhere and it's backward India. The shore guys took our cases up the jetty and put them on a trailer – and then hitched up a camel to it!

'I joined my next ship in Suva, Fiji, and from there we went down to Kwinana in Western Australia. From Kwinana we went to Auckland, and then it was to Aden via Colombo, and then from Aden to Bombay. We were in Bombay for quite a long time. It was one of those ships where, if anything was going to happen, then it did. After three weeks of repairs we tried to sail, and I remember being on the bridge with the pilot and measuring how far we'd got. It was 4 · 3 miles when we clapped out again. We had to anchor and start again.

'Eventually we did get to Dubai in the Gulf and the only thing that had worked without fail was the air conditioning – and then that packed up. We were there for about three weeks in the stifling heat. Then we went up to Basra, which was just before the war started between Iraq and Iran. The Shatt-al-Arab is very narrow, and going down river is a very slow business because you're always waiting for ships to swing on the tide. As it was, we scraped the bottom of the river going back down fully laden.'

These travels sound a great deal more exciting than they ever are to tanker crews. Ralph Chaplin, a young engineer in tankers, says, 'My job certainly does involve travel, but unfortunately it's mostly a case of seeing somewhere from the end of an oil jetty. I've seen a fair selection of oil terminals, but one in Curacao looks no more exotic than one in Belfast.

'After spending weeks getting somewhere the ship may be alongside for two days. During these two days you still have to maintain full watches. The oil jetty is invariably miles from anywhere, and with your off-duty time restricted to eight hours, some of which is normally spent asleep, your opportunities for seeing somewhere new are limited to a few quick photographs, a beer and a taxi back to the ship. In my last couple of trips the most I've had was a run ashore in Hamburg for four or five hours and one whole day ashore in Japan.'

Elizabeth Flynn and Ralph Chaplin have started their seafaring careers in trades that older men feel they have been reduced to. The young listen to the tales of their elders and have a good idea of what they have missed. Without being resentful they do nevertheless feel cheated by the relatively pedestrian lives they are obliged to lead. Chris Warlow, for example, is in his early twenties, does not feel himself deprived but equally has few expectations and talks of the voyage of his last ship as if he were a bus driver describing the stops along the route:

'I was on a 75,000 cubic metres LNG [liquid natural gas] carrier and she was really on a liner trade between three Japanese ports and Lumut in Brunei. It was a two-week round trip. It would take us about sixteen hours to load in Brunei, and you couldn't get ashore unless you were sick.

'From Lumut we went to either Chiba, which is on the opposite site of the bay from Tokyo, or to Yokohama. On this ship it was almost pinpoint timing. We'd arrive off Tokyo Bay at about eight in the morning and pick up the pilot. You'd steam in and dock at about ten. Then you'd have to cool down the shore lines with gas and start the discharge proper at about midday. The bus would go for shore at one o'clock and would be back at five. You'd finish cargo during the night, on the four to eight. The pilot would be on board by eight and you'd be leaving. It was a twenty-four-hour turn-round and then back to Lumut. I did four months on that ship, and that's the whole story, really.'

Despite the unlikely nature of their character and the berths they are obliged to use, gas carriers can nevertheless provide a sample of the old-fashioned seafaring life, because pumping rates are sometimes extraordinarily slow. Peter Hyde found several wholly unexpected bonuses when sailing on one of Bibby's gas carriers:

'Once, when we were in Cartagena, in Spain, it took us about ten days to discharge our cargo of about 30,000 tons of LPG. The storage tanks were up a hill and miles away, and as they filled up the back pressure built up for us to pump against. At one time we were discharging at only twenty-four tons an hour when our maximum was about 3,000 tons an hour. This suited us very well. It gave us time to have a day off and go and have a look at the country we were in in daylight. I had a couple of days off in Cartagena. It was Easter time and they had a big religious festival with people whipping themselves and doing penance and walking around in Ku Klux Klan outfits!

'Six weeks later, and after we had fetched a cargo from Ras Tanura in the Gulf, we were at a place called Ismit in Turkey. Going through the Dardenelles was really beautiful, one of the prettiest stretches I've ever seen. There was nothing at Ismit. It was very backward, but fortunately we were only about fifty miles from Istanbul. Four of us, two engine cadets and two juniors, went up to Istanbul by bus. Istanbul has to be the most interesting place I've ever visited. The bazaar was incredible. It's all laid in streets: streets for leather, streets for gold, streets for silver. The street for gold was unbelievable. When all the lights were on you could look down the streets and everything shone. It was like the Arabian Nights. This, for me, really was going abroad.'

By contrast, there was little glitter for Tony Hinks on his last ship. The *Barber Perseus* is a RO-RO with a round-the-world itinerary, but it is little more than a super-ferry:

'Let's take it from arriving in Norfolk, Virginia, which will be at about two in the morning, previously having had a four- to five-hour stand-by coming up river. About twenty minutes after getting alongside we'll have the ramp down. On this ship we can load five decks from the stern, and we can also load on to the main deck with cranes and gantries. Now by six we've got everything ready for the shoreside men to come in. At that point we'll have about an hour's break and after that we could be loading catering, engine-room and deck stores. When that's done we might have an hour on the quay, working from our stacker truck, painting the ship's side, and soon after that it could be time to be getting the ramp up and lashing down the containers on deck ready to be off. After six hours we could be sailing again.

'With the pilot aboard we might then be going up the Chesapeake Canal to Baltimore, and by the time we get there it will probably be in time to start work the next morning. We might only be *there* for two or three hours and then we would be off to New York to start work again. If you're outward, then when you leave New York it's across the Atlantic, through the Mediterranean, the Suez Canal and the Red Sea to Jeddah, which is the first port of discharge. After that it's a six-day passage to Dubai.

'Jeddah is the longest stop, with thirty-six hours, but you *never* get ashore, because you can't get a pass. In Dubai you'll have about five hours, and then it's Dammam. You have a day in Dammam, and then over to Bahrain, where you usually have a night. From Bahrain we'll go up to Kuwait. After that we'll have an eight-and-a-half-day passage across the Indian Ocean to Singapore.

'In Singapore we'll be loading as well as discharging, whereas in the Gulf ports we'll have been discharging and picking up empties. Singapore is the first loading port for the States, but we'll only be there for about twelve hours. You could arrive there at ten at night and they'll be working the ship immediately. We'll be leaving at eleven the next morning, and then exactly the same could happen when you get to Hong Kong. You might have a bit longer in Hong Kong but you'll never get a day.

The next port is Keelung, in Taiwan, and then it's Kao-hsiung, and then it's off to Kobe in Japan. After Japan it's eleven and a half days across the Pacific to Los Angeles. We'll have about ten hours there, then it's down through the Panama, and at Cristobal at the Caribbean end of the canal we'll probably have a night in. Our next port is at Palm Beach in Miami, and then we'll go up to Savannah, Baltimore and New York, and then we'll go back round the coast to New Orleans, Houston, Norfolk, Baltimore, New York and then off to Jeddah again.'

Tony Hinks spent six months on that ship and never once had time to go ashore. No wonder that he says, 'I would never advise anyone to go to sea now, because they're never going to find out about a proper seaman's life. In my short time at sea I've been quite fortunate – I've had ships where they were in port for several days, even a week, at a time but those ships are a thing of the past now. A young feller might get to all these good ports in the States, the Far East, Australia, but all he's going to see is the dock. My last ship I had six months away and eight hours ashore. That's not going to sea, is it?'

The same advice would certainly be offered by Colum Leggatt, who started at sea just in time – in the early 1970s, that is – to get a good taste of the old-style life in the cargo liners. 'Coming from a Catholic and grammar school background, I must say that Wellington was one of the great eye-openers of my life ... I think, going down to Australia or New Zealand on a meat boat then – well, everyone knows what that means. The people are incredibly hospitable. The names of the companies that ran the meat boats – Shaw Savill, NZS, Port Line, Blue Star – these were household names. Everyone knew what the funnel down in the port was; especially was this so in New Zealand and the smaller ports in Australia. In some of these smaller ports you're almost a sort of VIP and the ship coming in is a big thing ...'

But Colum Leggatt went to sea too late to get the full measure of what Tony Hinks calls the 'proper seaman's life'. The following account of his last voyage shows in many ways a sharper contrast between present and past, because the older men had enough experience to savour what people of Colum's age have merely tasted:

'My last voyage was on a 66,000 ton bulk carrier on a time charter to an American company, owned by C. Y. Tung of Hong

Kong and managed by Furness Withy, with British officers and a crew of Indians and Filipinos. We were on a run from the Gulf ports of the States – New Orleans, it was – to Japan with grain. The voyage back to the States was in ballast.

'I did four and a half months on it, so I did two voyages. We were running at twelve knots, so we spent, I should say, getting on for forty days between New Orleans and Japan. Altogether we'd be in the Mississippi river a week, though we'd load the ship in about two days. The rest of the time would be spent at anchor waiting for a berth, and then we lost a lot of time messing about with ballast to get under the bridges – we were having to pump it in and then pump it out again. Then we had to prepare the holds to take the grain.

'The main problem with the whole run was boredom. I think the first time we were in New Orleans most people got a run ashore, but then a lot of people were just prepared to go on the ship, get on with the job and get off four and a half months later. They weren't concerned with going ashore. At the other end we went to this place in Japan. In fact we were there for Christmas, but the berth we were on was a secure jetty, so we had to go in a launch from the outboard side into town, which was maybe an hour's boatride away. Discharging, we had almost five days and but for the berth we'd have had a good run ashore.

'If you're trying to get at what's gone out of the game, it's that sailing from home on a low and coming back on a high. You knew that if you were going off to the Caribbean or New Zealand you'd be back in, say, two or five months. There was a pay-off day and all that, and it was sort of happy memories of the voyage that you'd just finished. Now it's getting on a plane and you're thrust straight into your new environment and then when the magic day comes that you've marked off in your calendar you're dragged away again.

'I think if you asked any merchant seaman about any UK port he'd talk about it as if it was heaven, because most of us seem to get on jumbo jets at Heathrow and that's it for four or five months.'

Even on the cruise ships and in direct contradiction to what is offered in temptation in the brochures, there seems to be little glamour for the crews. Dino Livingstone, for example, has distinctly monochrome recollections of the *QE II*.

'It was all right. The ports were all right, but the main aim of that ship, apart from when it was running across the Atlantic, is cruising, and they want the passengers to spend as little time as humanly possible ashore so that they'll spend all their money on the ship. The thing with this is you're only in for eight hours and you're running around trying to have a good time and see a bit of the place and then you're running back to catch the ship. I've been to a lot of places, and I can show you where they are on the map, but I haven't got a clue what they look like.'

The coastal trade's fleet had its specialised ships in much the same way as the deep-sea fleet – passenger and cargo liners, tramps, liquid bulk carriers and so on. And then coasting, as we have seen, shaded off into what are called the short-sea trades and the middle trades: down the Biscay coast as far south as such Spanish ports as San Sebastian and Santander, northward to Norway and the Soviet arctic ports in summer, eastward into the Baltic. The coastal and middle trades have been affected by some of the same forces that have wrought such far-reaching changes on life in the deep-sea ships: containerisation and the RO-RO ship transformed the liner trades by eliminating most of the ships on the routes across the North and Irish Seas. And then road transport has killed off virtually all the small and specialised liner services that linked the small and out-of-the-way places with the city ports.

Those seamen who are left working in the smaller ships are in the tankers carrying refined oil products; the gas and chemical carriers running from the wharves and jetties of the chemical plants of Teeside and Merseyside; the tramps carrying such bulk cargoes as coal, grain and quarry products. It is the bulkers which predominate in the middle trades ....

Jack Isbester works for a Norwegian firm, Jebsen's, and has spent most of the last four years working in the European trades. 'Jebsen's have more than a hundred contracts for the transportation of dry bulk cargoes between European ports and employ some twenty-five ships in the trade under the Norwegian, British, French, German and Icelandic flags, along with chartered-in tonnage as necessary. A contract might be for as little as two or three cargoes a year or for as many as twenty or thirty. The trade tends to focus on Norway, but there are many voyages which don't touch that country. Cargoes typically take one day to load and two days to discharge, and sea passages are usually about two days long. Between early July and the beginning of September 1983 my voyages have been:

Mo-i-Rana, Norway	*to*	Sauda, Norway	*with*	coke
Jossingfjord, Norway		Szczecin, Poland		ilmenite
Helsingborg, Sweden		Nordenham, Germany		iron oxide
Bremen, Germany		Odda, Norway		coke
Mongstad, Norway		Rotterdam, Holland		coke
La Coruna, Spain		Holla, Norway		quartz
Mo-i-Rana, Norway		Porsgrunn, Norway		coke
Helsingborg, Sweden		Nordenham, Germany		iron oxide

July and August are the slack periods in Europe, and we spent five days at anchor during July and four days at buoys in Rotterdam during August.' That is a very typical trading pattern for a ship of its sort, and – at least as measured in breathlessness – differs little from Matt Bainbridge's chemical carrier:

'The ones I'm on only trade to northern Europe, though on the odd one you might go down to the Mediterranean. The one I'm on has never been further south than Lisbon or more north than Norway and sometimes into the Baltic. We have no specific run. Sometimes we might go up the Manchester Ship Canal to Ellesmere Port but more often than not it's Middlesbrough or Grangemouth. It might be Immingham but then it might be Antwerp or Le Havre. You could take a cargo to or from any of these places. You never stop running. Those ships never stop for breath, although they're only about 2,000 tons. They can pump in about eight or nine hours, though that's if it's a full load. Sometimes you'll take a tankful to one port and another tank to another port.

'If the cargo is benzine, then we'd probably load that at Middlesbrough and take it to Le Havre. Sometimes, the way it looks to us, we'll take a load to Le Havre, discharge it, wait a day and then load it back again. Just a month ago, to take an example, we loaded nitrile at Middlesbrough. We took it to Antwerp, but on the way we stopped at Rotterdam to exchange papers to show that it had apparently come from the Soviet Union. This took two hours. We went into the port, never discharged the cargo, then took it to Antwerp and pumped it ashore. Then we reloaded it and took it back to Middlesbrough. It's about tax, isn't it?'

The sort of life described here by Jack Isbester and Matt Bainbridge has been familiar enough – though presumably without the tax avoidance bit – to the men of coastal tankers for many, many years. But still working on the coast, just as there are deep-sea, are a lot of seamen who once and not so very many years ago lived a far more relaxed if hard-working existence. One coastal master recalls, as an example, his early years on tiny coasters:

'There's plenty of little ports up around the Western Isles that I used to go into quite a lot. Now Oban was a place I always liked. I think they call it the "Gateway to the Highlands". Then there was Portree, a little port way up there in Skye. In days gone by, when I was working up there for Gardiner's, we were taking general cargo of all sorts of stuff – it could be bags of sugar, bags of flour – and you could be doing as many as twelve or fourteen little places. We could be in Port Ellen in Isla and Port Askey up in the Sound of Isla. I think there were two distilleries there then, so you could be collecting the big kegs of whisky to take to Glasgow to get bottled. Maybe you've read *Para Handy*? It was pretty much like that.'

Tom Calder, on the other hand, lived what might appear to be a much more cosmopolitan existence. 'We used to take this ship over to Rouen and then up the Seine to Paris. The *Vauban* used to run out of London, and then there was the *Marne* and the *Somme* that used to run out of Queen's or Canning Dock, here in Liverpool. We'd spend a day in Rouen and then it was up river to Paris. We used to tie up to the banks at night because the pilots would only go up in daylight. We'd take a general cargo over – it might be whisky and chocolate for Paris, and we might bring a cargo of grain from Rouen. Going up the Seine to Rouen from picking up the pilot would take about sixteen hours and going up the Seine to Paris could take three days, though it depended on the time of year, and then you could get held up by the bridges. In Paris we might only get a couple of hours, but as a rule you'd get a night in. It was quite a nice sight, going up that river with all the vineyards on both sides.'

With spending so much time in port the coastal seaman might be expected to get to know places in a way that would be unusual for the deep-sea people. In fact, however, coastal men have tended to see ports in much the same light, and once ashore headed for much the same institutions. As a coastal skipper said, 'At one time I used to run regularly to London, and I thought I knew London, but it wasn't until me and the wife had a fortnight's holiday there that I did know London. But before that I'd been trading back and forth to the various jetties in the London river and you just went to the first village that was there and then probably into the first bar, picture house, dance hall or whatever the case might be.' Here in this observation, albeit carefully coded, is what is called 'a decent run ashore' without which a 'proper seaman's life' is not possible.

II

Little skill and less imagination are needed to decode the expression 'a decent run ashore'. Furthermore, the activities concealed do not always have to be pursued ashore. A thirty-five-year old ship's cook said without any inhibition that Bangkok was a marvellous place: 'It's brilliant, it's fantastic, you have a great time. Everyone from the Old Man down with a bird on board. They weren't allowed on the wharf. They came out on the river in taxi boats, like a Mama-san with eight girls in each boat. There'd be about six or seven boats and you just throw cargo nets down and up they come.'

A great deal of shipboard talk is about ports and the sort of time that might be bad in them. The longer the passage the more the talk, until the air might be dense with expectation among the younger and less experienced crew members when arrival is imminent. Tacitly encouraged by the extravagant reminiscing of the older hands, the young are anxious to get their 'badges' of membership. What the literal-minded young miss in these ritual braggings of past deeds with women and drink is a nuancing of self-mockery. In mistaking the public affirmation for the private performance, the young seaman does not immediately learn that their conception of the ultimate male is no more nor less substantial than other rhetorics. Convinced that reality exists as described, they go looking for it. This, after all, is part of what they have come away for; come to try out for themselves those stories they have heard from lads six months older who have come back full of the 'good runs ashore' they had wherever it was. It is the sort of story now told by Frank Fearon, who laughs at himself as he was on his first trip in 1965 when he was sixteen and only just out of school:

'It was about Christmas in Valaparaiso, and here they loved the English people. Nobody had any money – they'd run out, and the captain wouldn't give them a sub, so we started selling marmalade and anything else we could get our hands on. Well, around Christmas Day we were skint again, so I seized this big Christmas cake that the cook had made for the officers. It was a three-tier job and it must have taken him about three months to make it. I saw this cake in the saloon, so I got a pillow case, put it over the top and took it ashore to this bar where all the seamen gathered, called Jaco's Bar, and that's where all the women were whose job was entertaining the seamen.

'I walked in without a penny in my pocket but with this pillow case with the cake in it. I put it on the bar and said it was the 'signorita's cake'. I couldn't go wrong after that. I was four days in that bar with all the women and free ale and the seamen with me were getting free ale as well. Of course, when we got back to the ship there was nothing down for me and I got logged quite a few days' pay.

'I'd stayed ashore for four days. I was in the bar all day and then at night one of the women would take me back to her little flat. When I got home and told my friends what had happened they wouldn't have it, they thought I was telling a load of lies. But if you were a kid down there with blue eyes you couldn't go wrong with women. I mean, that was all you wanted when you were sixteen, wasn't it? Women about the age of thirty! I mean, that wasn't done in Liverpool, was it?'

Actual performance of the classic male role is far less important than its observance. This is neatly revealed in Ralph Chaplin's account of his first run ashore, which was in Curacao. 'I was being led up to expect something special from that place – it was all 'nudge, nudge, wink, wink' and that sort of stuff. About two hours before we got in I was down below and the second engineer came up to me and said I'd better get out of there and get changed ready to go ashore. He told me that if I stayed on board he'd keep me working, but otherwise I could be off, as long as I was back before sailing. As soon as the gangway was down we were off, and twenty-eight hours later we came back – well, actually, it wasn't that long. We crept back on board at three in the morning for a few hours' sleep and disappeared ashore in Willemstadt before the second got up and found us. We didn't get too drunk or anything, but we had to stay ashore, because they'd have taken the mickey out of us something rotten if we hadn't.'

In the legends that seafarers inherit and then reconstruct when they weave again into the same cloth fragments of their own experience and that of 'one bloke I sailed with', tales of heroic drinking rank higher than those of sexual activism. This is partly because drinking is often the only possible form of social activity in a strange place and partly because it is the most uncomplicated and undemanding way of showing yourself to be a 'good lad'. We can see aspects of all these elements in Tony Santamara's candid recall of his early months at sea:

'There I am, hardly left school and sitting in a bar in Havana drinking Bacardi and Coke and sitting next to Castro soldiers who had their carbines with them. Many a time I got drunk with them, although of course I got drunk a lot quicker than them! I remember one of our down-below fellers, a Cingalese, coming back the worse for drink, and he was effing and blinding Castro and really giving Castro down the banks. He got locked up for that, though I don't know what he was charged with, but he got fined a hundred dollars and a couple of days in prison. Anyway, he came back with tales of wonder with what a fantastic gaol that was, that he could even have a woman in there.

'I think there must have been a lot of bravado about drinking and proving yourself to be a man but I can't honestly remember any of that at the time. But unless you went ashore in the afternoon there was nowhere else you could go ashore except to the bars and the cantinas. If you had the afternoon off, then you'd go ashore on your own because on my ship the catering was only a small department. Then you might do a bit of walking around but you didn't really get into the cultural aspects, the historical things, seeing how people live, and all that – and you'd inevitably end up in a bar. It's only in the last ten years that I started to take an interest in the places we visited, and I've tried to get the young kids interested but they don't really want to know, or if some of them do show an interest it'll only be in a wayward way and they'll end up on the ale just like I did. There's very few of them don't.'

It was only a matter of months after being tied up in Havana that Tony's ship was in Mauritius and he was putting in for a £20 sub '... because in Mauritius you could have a suit made in a day for less than £5, and then, you could get lovely shirts, a lot of French stuff, and it was really a boss port ...'

Ports that could be nominated as 'boss' or providing a 'good run ashore' were those enabling seafarers, especially the young, a comprehensive opportunity to live out the part that tradition required. So the ideal place was one that had a hugely favourable exchange rate, low levels of purchase tax, and where things were so absurdly cheap that a working-class lad, temporarily liberated from the economic restrictions of his class, could cut a bit of a dash and even be something of a superior person. Expressive of this was John Dooligan's comment that 'You only needed £2 in Chile and you were a millionaire.' Another seafarer commented of that part of the world:

'It was a good place for Jack ashore all the way down that coast. Valparaiso in Chile was just about everyone's favourite port, though Callao in Peru wasn't too bad either. In fact they were all all right, really. We never had much money then, but then, down there you didn't need a lot. I remember one time when an older feller and I used to go ashore in Callao when there were eighty *soles* to the pound and you could get a rum and Coke, in one bar we knew, for three! You were dead drunk for about 25p! Mind, I wouldn't say the rum was of the best quality, but it was effective!'

Reminiscences of this sort are characteristic themes of yarning in the officers' and crew's bars of today's ships. With a good spread of ages in a ship's crew you could construct a history of the movement of exchange rates for every major and many minor currencies since 1945.

A good port had to have a number of qualities, but first and above all it had to be cheap: you had to be able to enjoy a standard of living that was out of reach at home. Barney Moussa has some devastating things to say about the attitude of mind and the self-deceptions that are involved in these calculations:

'There's no such a thing as a good ship. There's just places where they go that you can have a good time and forget the ship! There are good ports. And a good port is the place where you spend all your money, because you're foolish when you go ashore.

'Now I've been to a place called Tahiti and it's a poor country.

That's one thing I can't understand – why we and other people from Western countries think that place is beautiful. If you come to my country, in East Africa, you get everything just the same – we've got coconut trees, we've got cheap labour who'll work all day for nothing to rip down the coconuts. But it's cheap and for we seamen it's cheap drink, cheap women – so it's a beautiful place.

'In Tahiti if you're English people or German people they come on board ship and put flowers round your neck. Such a thing they don't get in other countries, so they think this is a special place. Then you can get married in Tahiti – it's one-night love. So the seaman can always tell you about the good ship because it went to the good port. But when he gets on board ship he changes from his good suit into his dirty clothes and he's just a slave, cheap labour – and that's what we are, cheap labour. We are just opportunists.'

Barney Moussa is right. Seafarers are opportunists, and in any port that is not attached to one of the wealthier nations it is absurdly easy, in sensuous pursuits, for the underdog to become an overdog for a day and a night. But then, on the other hand – and Tommy Keefe is a good example – a visit to a 'good port' can also be an exercise in political education. 'It opened up my eyes, opened up new horizons, to see, for example, the way other people were living. When I was in some of the Third World countries I just couldn't believe what I saw. In Caracas, in Venezuela – such a nice country, and such nice people, but so many oppressed. I think what got me politically-minded the way I am now was seeing so much wealth and then the way so many people were suffering, the conditions they were living in. We used to employ on the ship somebody who would just take the scraps. You'd take the ''rosey'' out to them after it was used, and things like that.'

Many other seafarers also have political experiences and these, too, pass into folklore, become part of the collective legend and thus part of the seafarers' self-image wherein they figure as broad-minded cosmopolitans who have seen a thing or two and know about the nastiness of the world. Frank Williams, born to a Barbadian mother and a black American father in Liverpool, was none too impressed with Savannah in Alabama:

'It's still bad down there, you know. I was the only black guy

on the ship, and I went ashore with about eleven of the crew and
we all went into this bar, the nearest to the dock. We were all
stood up there at the bar and the barmaid was at the back when
we went in. When she appeared a few minutes later her eyes
nearly popped out of her head when she saw me – I thought there
was something strange because as we walked in all the heads were
turning but I wasn't sure whether they were looking at me.
Anyway, she said, ''We don't allow blacks in here.'' That really
took me by surprise, because being born in Liverpool I wasn't
used to anything as blunt as that, it's usually more subtle.

'The guys with me just said they weren't staying if they
weren't serving me, and we all went out and down the road to
the next club, where we all went in without any hassle. Later on
we were going into this shop for a take-away and I was just going
to walk in when the woman said she wouldn't serve me if I went
in. When that happens you feel you're being repressed and it just
makes you want to lash out because people are so stupid.'

Hermon McKay from an older generation never even bothered
to go ashore in the southern ports of the USA. 'I wouldn't go near
New Orleans, for obvious reasons. The bars were on then and I
know that in situations like that I'm going to get into trouble,
so to save that I wouldn't go ashore in places like that. I'm not
going to put up with being insulted and I'm not going to put
myself in a position where I know I'm going to be insulted, so
I take the line of least resistance.'

Andrew Milligan had an involuntary view of the sort of circumstances that Hermon McKay and Frank Williams have been sub-
jected to, albeit in what was then a Portuguese colony. He recalls
'... sitting in the square in Lobito, in Angola. There were four or
five of us having beer in the evening, and there was an oldish
negro working there as a shoeshine boy doing the shoes of a
Portuguese boy who must have been about fourteen or fifteen.
The boy threw a few escudos on the pavement and the negro
shrugged his shoulders and held out his hands as if to say it wasn't
enough. The boy told him to go but the old man repeated his
gestures and the boy kicked him in the chin ... I thought to myself
at the time that maybe the Portuguese would have trouble – and
they did in the end.'

And then Mick Hunter found himself unwillingly caught up
in Zimbabwean politics in 1966 when the white Rhodesians

declared themselves independent and were then blockaded. Mick was ashore in Beira, Mozambique, and got badly beaten up by white Rhodesians:

'One of the worst experiences I've ever had at sea was when I was on the *Kenya Castle* in Beira at the time of the Rhodesian crisis. We went ashore with two or three Scotsmen and we weren't bothering anyone, just sitting there drinking quietly, and we weren't drunk or anything. Suddenly these Rhodesians burst into the bar and they asked if we were English – and then things happened so fast that it was every man for himself. There were too many of them for us and they started kicking and beating us. I managed to crawl under the table and then legged it out of the bar, trying to get away. I ran down this street but it was a cul-de-sac and they caught me and beat me again, they were kicking me while I was in the gutter.

'I had the sense to pretend that I was knocked out and then a Portuguese copper came up but he didn't want to bother the Rhodesians – they were all fascists together. I lay there moaning and groaning and making out I was much worse than I was, and then two of them got worried and picked up two of us and took us back to the dock gates and dumped us there.'

What rankled with Mick Hunter, and indeed still does, was that the ship's captain decided that he'd been drunk and causing trouble and logged him a day's pay. 'At the time I felt like writing to the papers about this. Here I was getting beaten up while all this Rhodesian trouble was on – and then getting punished as well! Here was this arrogant man blaming us, and we hadn't done anything at all. He was telling us we must have been drunk and it must have been us who caused the trouble. That was a *classic* of the attitude.'

It would be an exceedingly unusual seafarer who would deliberately try to engage in local politics. And on those occasions where the odd individual might try, it would tend to be gestural. A case in point here is that of a seaman who, during the period of the infamous colonels in Greece, smuggled in anti-Junta leaflets and then threw them out of the window of a coach travelling between Athens airport and Piraeus. In an earlier period there were of course seamen who fought in the International Brigade in Spain, and there was one British merchant seaman, Albert Cole, who was in the Republican navy. Earlier again, it was common enough for seamen to desert in the ports of Peru and Chile to serve in the ships of the respective navies. In more recent years, however, seafarers were usually bystanders in Latin American ports. Andrew Milligan, for example, always enjoyed going to Buenos Aires. But, while he found it a beautiful place, he also found it frightening in recent years:

'I remember one Sunday afternoon when it was popular among ship's personnel to go to the cinema, have a meal and then perhaps go to another movie. On this afternoon the government "hit squad", or call it what you will, came along in their vehicles, and I remember everyone on the street turning away from them to look in shop windows. This smacked of something intangibly sinister. Then there were always the tales of people being gaoled for no apparent reason, people off the ships too. We had a passenger once whose husband was one of the "disappeared ones" and she told me that two or three of her husband's friends had disappeared as well. But in Buenos Aires this wasn't something people wanted to talk about too much. They'd fob you off or change the subject if they didn't know you too well.'

Parts of West Africa, on the other hand, are places where private enterprise and lack of State control receive almost perfect expression. Janis James is a regular visitor to that part of the world and has developed quite a jaundiced view of what is to be found there:

'In some ports we've had bogus customs officers come aboard the ship, go through the bond and take what they wanted, and then ten minutes later we've had more "customs officers" come aboard and again they've taken exactly what they wanted. You just never know who is what and who is whom, with just anybody coming and demanding this stuff. At one stage in one particular area it was company policy that if you didn't have a pilot to take you straight from the anchorage to the port, then you didn't go, because we were forbidden to anchor in the river in transit.

'Off certain villages and towns, if you're in a ship with a low freeboard, people could get aboard from canoes, and there have been attacks even with sub-machine guns. It's getting really serious down there. Even twenty-five miles off Lagos a little Dutch ship was just drifting rather than at anchor and she got attacked and the cook was very badly cut up.'

Despite the first-hand and close second-hand experiences, despite the opportunities to inquire into and examine popularly held views about other people and other countries, it is surprising how *in*curious most seamen are about the places they visit. Going ashore is less an 'expedition of discovery' and more a search for a substitute for the Saturday-night-out of people who live and work ashore. And then seamen in ports of other countries, just like many people abroad on holiday, feel free to behave in ways akin to those of an army of occupation. Seafarers, however, unlike tourists, take a little bit of home with them.

Seafarers never visit a foreign country in circumstances where they are completely abroad, where they are obliged to adjust quickly and then adhere to the customs of those who are native. Down in the port there is that ship with a red ensign flying over the stern, the English language and three British meals a day. The seafarer can avoid being a stranger, can remain completely British by going back to 'Britain' after a few hours ashore. Cocooned in this British community wherever they go, it is not surprising that you can often hear it said that 'one port is much the same as another'.

The milieu of the ship, and the social performances required of crew members, who are unable to live as isolates, conspire to discourage curiosity and adventurousness. Young people, almost unknowingly, get drawn into unseeing ways and can soon become extraordinarily blasé and drawn into the seen-it-all-before sentiments of saloon and messroom. Joining a ship in Suva, Fiji, and after less than twelve months at sea, one young officer cadet said, 'I was getting a bit fed up with exotic places – but I liked Australia and New Zealand.'

These are typical and recurrent sentiments, and it is remarkable how often seafarers, when asked about ports and places, offer accounts that relate to their first or second trip and thereafter have poor recollections. But they will remember Australian and New Zealand ports, especially the latter. Here at least there are cultural similarities and identities, and so the adjustments that have to be made in these countries are negligible: in Melbourne and Wellington it is possible to be British outside the dock gates.

A leisurely indulgence in many of the shoregoing experiences described here is a thing of the past. One consequence, as we saw at the beginning of this chapter, is that in those parts of the world where rules and their enforcers are for sale like any other commodity, aspects of the 'good run ashore' have become portable and available for temporary installation aboard ship. Elsewhere, and for the seafarers who are left, the 'good run ashore', where it is to be had at all, is something to be snatched, to be taken on the run like a hamburger or a packet of peanuts. Gone too are the possibilities of tiring of Valparaiso and deciding that the next trip will be down to Aussie for a slice of home away from home. The reduction of the typical port turnaround time to the pattern of the tanker and the location of terminals for boxes and bulk cargoes miles away from town or city has made the seaman dependent upon specially provided bus or boat services. Going ashore to timetable like a commuter is a different world away from a ship literally tied up to a tiny one-street port in remoter Australia or an exciting short taxi ride from Manhattan, New York.

For the seaman in his early forties, grown out of the impulsion to dive into the 'first and last', there are few opportunities to develop new-found curiosities. Tony Santamara would like to make good some of his past: 'I'd love to go away to sea again, but what I'm doing now is just a job. Now I just go between Heysham and Douglas and I don't go away to sea. I'd love to be able to do a three-month trip again, but on the other hand I don't want to leave my family too much. Looking at it from a selfish point of view, what would be ideal would be nine months on this job – pretending, this is – and a three-month trip every year. I'd like to go down to Madagascar, for example, to see what it's like now that it's the Malagasy Republic. I didn't see as much as I should have done when I was there, so I'd like to go back.'

But there is no going back, neither for Tony Santamara nor for anyone else. In this new epoch of seafaring the gap between what he would like and was once possible and what is now attainable cannot be bridged.

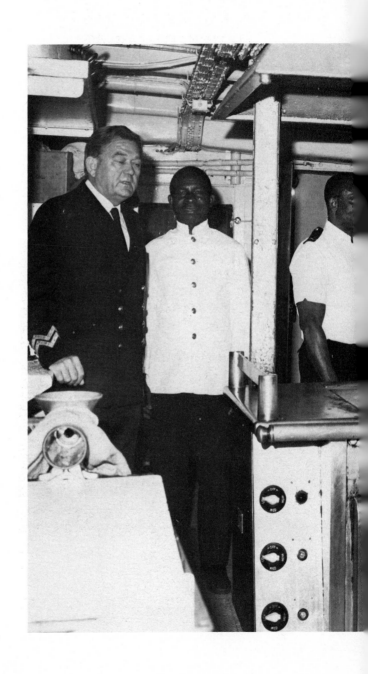

[VI] · *Hierarchy*

When first I was a foremast man I often did pretend
That if ever I got promoted I would be a seaman's friend;
When in a little time I got to be a mate,
I then like many others soon forgot my former state;
When I became a captain I thought myself a king,
And very soon forgot the foremast man I'd been.

Anon.

Hierarchy touches almost every aspect of shipboard life. It is a subject which generates a lot of heat among seafarers, reveals deep-running social divisions and, in this respect at least, seems to offer a microcosm of society at large.

The sharpest antagonisms concern the quality of the relationship between officers and crew, although it is rare for anyone to question the existence of a hierarchy based on technical skill. Indeed, because ships are such dangerous places, a high degree of technical competence in officers commands respect and even admiration. What is vehemently and angrily contested is the tendency of officers to clothe professional skills in pretensions to superior personal worth. A large part of this chapter is taken up with showing how these claims to superiority are made, have been developed and encouraged, and are resisted.

This chapter also deals with those conflicts which have less to do with rank and more to do with inherited ideas as to whether different types of work are 'manly', 'menial' or 'proper seafaring'. With regard to these definitions there are disputes as to the relative status of mates, engineers, pursers and catering officers. Similar conflicts are found within the crew. The ABs sometimes see themselves as the *real* seamen, whereas cooks and stewards are seen as doing menial work. If there is a large engine-room crew a third dimension is added: greasers and motormen may do 'manly' work but it is not 'seamen's' work. The divisions of this kind are more or less pronounced according to the size and type of ship: a cruise liner with a crew of eight hundred obviously provides a much larger set of possibilities than a coastal tramp with a crew of eight.

The evaluations placed upon different types of work have effects upon the general nature of relations between officers and crew. Within each department, officers and ratings meet on face-to-face terms and have to find ways of co-operative working.

This co-operation at work may then form the basis of a certain departmental solidarity which is fostered and deepened by the knowledge of how members are judged by other departments. The alliances thus formed between officers and ratings *within* departments help to ensure that, in the everyday work of the ship as a whole, 'officers' and 'crew' rarely make an appearance as two straightforwardly opposed groups.

If the division of labour needed to move ships around coasts and across oceans modifies and mutes social antagonisms, the solidarity of seafaring also plays a part. Seafarers of all ranks share the same disruptions and frustrations, the same isolation, the same hazards. The sense of a sharing in the same cloth that comes from these common experiences always extends the hope and the opportunity of realising a less divisive shipboard society.

I

It is a general rule in industry and commerce that the more elaborate the division of labour, the more complicated the hierarchy. That this is the case also in merchant ships is seen clearly in Jim O'Kane's account of his move from a coaster to a deep-sea tanker in 1959:

'Going on a Shell tanker was a bit like going from a vifllage to a small town. On the Shell tanker it was better everything. Better food, better accommodation, better money. But there was a lot of bullshit. I went from a small ship where you were just part of nine men, but on the tanker you were separated; you were down aft, and that was it. The only dealings you had with anybody up amidships was when you were at the wheel on watch.

'When you went on the wheel the mate on the watch would just give you your course and that was it; you might as well not be there. You couldn't smoke when you were up there on the wheel but he could smoke up there in the wheelhouse. I couldn't figure this out for a long time. But after I got into the way of it, once I'd worked out the way things were, it didn't seem strange at all. They were the officers and we were the workhorses, and that was it. This is the way deep-water is. I suppose it's these who class themselves better than you when they've got these tickets. It's the middle class and the working class.'

On the *Ann M*, Jim O'Kane's coastal tramp, there might have been something of a rough-and-ready equality at work, but even on this ship the mates and engineers did not share their mess or their TV with the cook and the ABs, although there were only nine in the total crew. There might be a big ship and a small ship attitude, but on the small bulk carriers that Colum Leggatt had sailed on '... we sat on one side of the galley and they sat on the other and you could see across and even ask for their mustard! But I don't think either side wanted to mix.'

These separations on small ships reach proportions that seem absurd but which seafarers find quite natural. On one of Eric Knowles's ships there was a crew of twelve but the same film had separate showings for officers and crew, and on Barry Roberts's North Sea supply boat '... the only TV is in the crew's mess and when you go in there you do pick up a change in the atmosphere'. In point of fact the 'togetherness' of the small ship is commonly overstated, and even idealised, but compared with the passenger liner it does seem almost communal.

In generous mood a seafarer might concede that, on a passenger ship, officers in uniform are part of what the customers think they are paying for, but it is also officer behaviour on passenger ships which attracts either the strongest condemnation or the sharpest ridicule. Dino Livingstone found things on the *QE II* a bit comic: 'A lot of what goes on aboard ship in the name of discipline is a bit juvenile really, it's quasi-military. Now I was never logged on there but I was on the bridge doing jobs some-times when people were getting logged. There were the masters-at-arms, retired policemen, standing to attention there ... it was sort of Gilbert and Sullivan, Star Chamber stuff. I thought it was a bit ludicrous. And there was the way they wore their uniforms on there – for me, it was like play-acting.'

The use of ritual and the adoption of special forms of dress to create a certain theatricality are commonly used methods of enforcing hierarchy. The resort to theatrical practices as a means of asserting power and authority is especially clear in courts of law. It is, therefore, of more than passing interest to hear Tony Santamara describe his encounter with the system of adminis-tering justice in the Union Castle Line:

'My relationships with officers on the passenger boats were generally good. I was always industrious, so I didn't have any problems – until I went on the Union Castle boats. There it was the full-on class distinction, and I've never seen anything like it.

I remember it was in 1973 on the *Windsor Castle*, and it was like the lions and the gladiators – them being the lions and us the gladiators. They'd have you up on the bridge for the pettiest thing, and they'd all be up there. It *seemed* like twenty of them in their full regalia. Now I've never seen it but I've heard people say that they'd have the union jack on the skipper's desk! They'd go to the most elaborate lengths to get you; they'd conspire and tell lies to do you.

'I was a waiter and nightwatchman on the *Windsor Castle* while the ship was on the South African coast. Part of my job was that every hour I had to take a tray of sandwiches up to the bridge for the officers. Now one time I went to the pantry to get the sandwiches and found that someone had stolen them, so I had to go down to the galley to get the sandwiches made, only to find that it was locked and the pantrymen off somewhere. It took me half an hour to get those sandwiches.

'I had to be up there on the hour for the same officer and then I might find that he hadn't eaten the last lot but I still had to have them up there just the same. Anyway, I'm on my way up there and I bumped into this master-at-arms, who said to me, 'Where have you been, boy?' and I asked him, 'Who are you calling "boy"?' Then he said I was half an hour late and so I told him what had happened. He told me I was drunk. I denied it, though I had had a drink – but then, there was no reason why I shouldn't have had. But he *was* drunk. Then he told me that he was knocking me off, and I told him that only a catering officer could do that and that I was going up to the bridge.

'When I got up there I explained to the mate why I was late and he said he thought that what I said was reasonable. I asked the mate to write what had happened into the bridge incident book and then he added, 'In my opinion this man is sober and quite capable of carrying out his duties.' But they had me up on the bridge the next day.

'There was the usual crowd there with scrambled egg all over them. I denied the charge and said I wanted to call the mate as a witness, and then they adjourned it until the afternoon when the mate came in and completely retracted everything he'd promised me. They'd got into him, you see, but to cut a long story short, I was logged and fined a day's pay.

'On those ships you were nothing to them. You were really

beneath them, and they made that plain to you. They went to all these elaborate lengths not just to take £3 off me but to keep me in "my place" and to perpetuate themselves on their little island of class distinction. Union Castle was notorious for this; it was ruthless, and it was racial too, you know. Look where they were running to! To Cape Town, where they really believed in that sort of thing. You see, a lot of the officers and skippers in that company were Yarpies, and altogether that company really was wicked.'

Some confirmation of this account of the Union Castle ships comes from Captain Mike Johns, who, fresh from his apprenticeship, made his first trip as an officer in the *Pendennis Castle*. 'The masters on these ships seemed to be a bit like ogres – especially the Old Man on this ship, who was known as Logger Lewis. It seemed that, with him, no sooner had he seen a seaman on deck then he had to get him in the log book. Everyone walked around in fear and dread of this man, but for me, as fourth mate, it was easy enough to keep clear.'

In the autobiographical fragments we have just glanced over are illustrations of how the texture of hierarchy and the role of the officer is affected by the type of ship, the trade it is in and the practices of the company concerned. There are, of course, other factors affecting the performance of the officer role, and not the least of these are the differences in class background between mates and engineers. In this connection we find that it was the pretensions of young engineers that were most resented, and here Billy Kerrigan's reactions were typical. 'I know that the vast majority of them served their time in places like Harland & Wolff's, where they'd been making tea and the like, and the next thing they appeared on the ships, and this bit of uniform seemed to go to their heads and the ground had disappeared from under their feet.'

Tony Santamara pursued the same theme and made an interesting contrast with the mates. 'Although they were from the same class as us, the same environment, these Glasgow engineers had just come from being can lads, from sitting on oily drums in the yard. But the next thing they were elevated to having a steward, to being served in the saloon with uniforms on.

'The mates seemed to be gentler with you, but looking back now I can see they were from a different environment. They were more distant with us in general, but they were easier to get on with than the engineer type who'd jumped out of his station. The mates were more distinctly different from us than the engineers, but in a working relationship they were more acceptable.'

In the engine room old hands like Jim Kierans would not tolerate those young engineers who tried to be officious. 'There are the juniors that break your heart, the ones who come ''I'm an officer''. They go around saying they're an officer and you'll do what they say. And you say to them, ''Why don't you fuck off?'' '

Jim Kierans's counterparts on deck, the bosun and the ABs, would not have the same problem with young and junior mates. These officers had served an apprenticeship *at sea*; they had learned the way 'things are done' aboard ship and probably had a second mate's ticket; they came from a middle-class background which gave them more self-confidence.

The system of training mates aboard working ships, perhaps after some preliminary training in school ships or nautical colleges, gave them a considerable head start over engineers of the same age when it came to knowing the rules of the game of officer behaviour. However, the style and mode of officer status had relatively little to do with the training and the background of deck officers. Far more critical were the economics of the liner trades on the old imperial routes and the availability of the Royal Navy as a model that could be emulated.

The liner companies tied the empire together by shifting its goods and ferrying its administrators. Sheltered by cartels on all the major imperial routes, firms like the P&O were able to give their officers conditions of service that often allowed them to live like gentlemen. It was the liner companies which set the pace and the style for others to emulate, and it was in them that the belief was encouraged that, although ships might carry the objects of commerce, shipping was really more of a service to the nation. The pride that was nurtured was in ships and nautical skills rather than in the efficient and expeditious movement of cargoes. To borrow the words of Humfrey Jordan, an ex-ship's officer and nautical novelist of the 1930s, business matters were a '... subject fit for owners but hardly proper for an officer'.[1] Echoes of some of these aspects of the liner companies are

contained here in John Curry's retrospective on joining his first
Clan Line ship in 1960:

'I was, as they say, "bright-eyed and bushy-tailed", green,
knowing absolutely nothing and, like others, absorbed the
traditions of the company. You heard about the masters who
went inshore of islands; of those who played safe and those who
didn't. You learned the traditions of other ships and you became
part of that tradition. I don't think many people really thought
much about the cargo you were carrying, other than the fact that
you had to go to various ports throughout the world with strange
and exotic-sounding names that themselves had a whole tradition
about what you could experience when you went ashore.'

Some further flavour of the Clan Line comes from Jack Isbester,
who was an apprentice in the company in the 1950s. Describing
an aspect of the afternoon routine, he says, 'At 1530 hours the
chief officer, clad in immaculate white, would tour the decks,
inspecting such work as could be viewed without getting dirty.
He would be accompanied by the Serang [Indian bosun], who
would also be impeccably clad in clean working clothes, and he
would have several assistants who were there to lift, move or open
anything which required any work or effort.' Jack Isbester also
recalls the '... commodore of Clan Line, who was a commodore,
RNR, entering the smoke room in which some fifteen of his officers were gathered. Two of the junior engineer officers failed
to leap to their feet at his entrance. He fixed them with a furious
glare and hissed at them, "Stand up when I come into the room!"
That was in 1954 on a ship which carried twelve passengers.'

After World War II company traditions were provided with a
heroic dimension as shipping firms memorialised the wartime
exploits of their ships by commissioning 'official histories'.
'Taffrail' (Captain Taprell Dorling), a then well known naval
writer, summarised his tribute to Blue Star:

... this war record of the Blue Star Line ... is a story of gallantry, endurance, fine seamanship and devotion to duty on the part of Merchant
Seamen. Nobody can read the accounts of those hard-fought convoys to
Malta; of an escape from Singapore in the full fury of the Japanese air
attacks; of the various voyages in open boats after ships had been sunk;
and of the cool bravery of officers and men in many differing circumstances of great peril and harship, without a thrill of pride and admiration
for the conduct and hardihood of those who fought at sea.[2]

Sentiments of this kind, amplified by the content of the official history and embellished by the stories passed on in oral legend, encouraged the belief, previously referred to, that to be a merchant seafarer was akin to being in the Royal Navy.

Company traditions were in fact merchant service or Merchant Navy traditions, for the values that were inculcated emphasised and celebrated the nobility of being a seafarer. Matters of commerce did not feature anywhere in educational and training programmes. Len Holder says of officers who started at sea in the 1950s and 1960s, 'From talking to seafarers of our generation at that time, you'd have thought they were working for philanthropic societies rather than for organisations that had to make profits to reinvest and survive.'

Only in exceptional circumstances did ships' masters book cargoes, and they knew little if anything about freight rates. It was true that a tramp master might be familiar with the various types of charter contracts and know a few dodges about how to squeeze in a few more tons of grain, but his job was essentially the same as that of a liner master: to load and discharge cargoes safely and deliver them undamaged between designated ports.

Working for a 'company' was not at all like working for a commercial enterprise. The company insignia in the badge on the officer's cap, on the silver buttons on the steward's white tunic, on the crockery and cutlery in mess and saloon; the company 'trade mark' in the architecture of the ships, in the colour scheme of the funnel, superstructure, masts and hull – all this livery and decorative display was simply a means of associating with a craft and an honourable tradition. The ultimate loyalty was not to a board of directors or to shareholders but to the practices of being a British seafarer.

In the more sheltered of the liner companies and especially among those where family influences continued, shipowners might themselves have a thoroughly non-commercial or even *anti*-commercial pride in ships and it sometimes showed in the way they built and decorated them. Until very recent years the family-owned Ben Line hired a Chinese crew member for little more than his ability to make external steel bulkheads look like wood-grained panels. In the 1960s there were still ships where every letter of the name and the port of registry had been cast in solid brass and where, in the first port of call after a long ocean

passage, men would be sent overside on stages to polish the
letters, pick out their edges in red paint and then laquer over the
top. Even in the late 1950s ships were still being build with that
degree of attention to cosmetic detail, and well into the 1970s
a director or general manager might be expected to visit a ship
soon after arrival in a UK port, know the captain by sight and
name, and cast a discerning eye over the ship's appearance.

The modern origins of encouraging officers to think themselves gentlemen and of building highly decorated ships lay in
the nineteenth-century development of fast passenger and mail
steamers. Shipowners then believed that a smartly turned out
ship, run with naval precision and observant of the niceties of
rank and status, might impress potential passengers and attract
shippers with precious cargoes to move.

From the very first, the P&O and the Royal Mail lines recruited
naval officers to senior positions and then encouraged their
civilian juniors and successors to model themselves on the naval
officer.[3] Ambitious officers, simultaneously attuned to their
employers' and to social aspirations of their own, took to obtain-
ing commissions in the Royal Naval Reserve and then spending
lengthy periods of training in warships.[4] Once this practice
became regular and widespread the shipping industry became a
merchant *service*, equipped with its own *corps d'élite*.

The apogee of the grand style came, like so much else British,
in the Edwardian years, and it is captured here in the loving
description of the departure of the Royal Mail Line's *Magdalena*
in 1905:

Her Captain, in frock coat, with the sunlight glinting on gold lace
about his sleeves and cap, was already waiting at the head of the
gangway. The officers in frock coats, and ship's company in No. 1
uniform, were fallen-in along the promenade deck. As the Commodore
and Marine Superintendant stepped on board the bos'n's pipe sounded
the 'Still'.

The Royal Navy couldn't have bettered the drill, nor the exercises
at boat and fire stations which followed. Every exhibition was timed by
Captain Hicks personally, who stood with open gold hunter in hand,
noting the officers' reports as they were made to the captain of the ship.
The *Magdalena* was due to sail on this bright Wednesday morning at
noon, with mails, a full complement of passengers, and her holds full
of special cargo for the West Indies and New York.[5]

Aping the Royal Navy to this degree was confined to the more luxurious of the passenger ships, and even there began to fall away after the First World War. Nevertheless, strong residues of the accompanying officer attitudes lingered on – as we have seen in Tony Santamara's encounter with the 'full-on class distinctions' of the *Windsor Castle*. The militarised management of hierarchy, as on ships like the *Magdalena*, completely disappeared in the straitened economic circumstances of shipping in the inter-war years, except on those ships with Asiatic crews. Officers elsewhere were left with the badges and perquisites of rank and little else, except the disciplinary provisions of the Merchant Shipping Acts. For those officers who cared enough about rank the 'logging session' provided a pretext to submit subordinate crew members to the impersonal and intimidating atmosphere of a uniformed and quasi-judicial court.

The use of the naval officer as a model by liner company officers was almost inevitable. There was the availability of a commission in the RNR; they wore a version of the Royal Navy uniform; they had helped run the nation's 'lifeline' in two world wars. Little wonder, then, that so many officers set their sights on the equivalent of RN status, and some, like Jack Isbester's commodore, tried to impose something of its style on a run-of-the-mill cargo liner. This does not mean, however, that among liner officers there was a conscious desire either to be, or to be like, a naval officer. Far more common was the unconscious assimilation of what being an RN officer meant into their idealised mental image of being an officer on a merchant ship.[6]

The extent of formality in shipboard social relations did not vary a great deal as between liner companies, but between them and the tramps there was quite a gulf. Here, for instance, is Noel Pereira drawing upon his experience as a Singapore pilot to compare practice in the tramps of the Bank Line with that in the liners of the Blue Funnel: 'On Blue Funnel it was all uniforms and peaked caps – the Old Man always wore a hat on the bridge, and the mate would always go forward with a hat on. But in Bank Line you could go on the bridge and everyone would be in civvies, and the only way you knew who the Old Man was when he presented himself to you. In Blue Funnel you never had that ambiguity as to which was the Old Man. He had four stripes on his shoulder and the gold braid on his hat.'

Relationships between officers and other crew members were correspondingly more relaxed on tramps but the divisions were there and understood just the same – it was just that they were expressed without the uniformed displays of rank. Tramps were more basic in their construction, in the extent of their decoration and in the conditions of living and working for officers. It was, therefore, very unusual for liner-trained officers to move into tramps and very common for tramp-trained officers to move into liners. The direction of officer mobility within the merchant fleet merely confirmed what everyone knew: that it was the liner firms which offered the best available means of enjoying officer status.

If ideas of what being an officer meant were produced through associations with the Royal Navy and the sheltered trading conditions for the liner companies, they were sometimes compounded by the social relations of the imperial connection. The term 'coolie-boat master' was often used by European members of the crew to refer to officers who had been accustomed to sailing with crews of Asian or African origin. Hermon McKay, being a black Liverpudlian, was well placed to know what the term meant:

'It was the officers you had problems with. To them you were even less than the ordinary crew members who were white. I had a double problem, especially with those who'd been with African, Indian or Chinese crews. When you got some of them coming on a ship, particularly deck officers who'd been in Bank Line or Bibby's or Brocklebank's with Indian crews, they'd try it on at first by calling you in a certain way, perhaps by clapping their hands. But they wouldn't do this with white crew members. After all, many of the mates had been used to white quartermasters and they'd been treated like members of the Master Race as well.'

One of the consequences of hiring crews from a variety of world regions has been a long-running debate as to the relative merits of seafarers with different ethnic backgrounds. Retired shipmasters who regularly sailed with Asiatic crews but who also had experience with Europeans could rarely resist making comparisons in which the latter fared unfavourably. Here, for example, is Captain D. G. O. Baillie, a former P&O commodore, comparing British with Lascar crews at the end of World War II:

There were endless disputes to be settled among the crew, who, compared with our peaceable Lascars, seemed to live in a perpetual ferment of disagreement either with each other or with me ...[7]

On his next ship Captain Baillie had a Lascar crew again:

... how thankful I was to see their neat uniforms, their smiling faces, and the efficient way they went about their work! And how aggreeable I found it to be looked after once more by a deft and cheerful Goanese steward who knew how to press my clothes, wait at table, and put on a white cap-cover properly![8]

A rather condensed and contemporary comparison is provided by Noel Pereira. 'On the British ships permanently based in the Far East the officers were accustomed to working with Chinese crews, and they had a completely different relationship with their crews than a British officer would have with a white crew. If you were the mate and down on the wharf with your bags, then you could send for the bosun to send down a couple of men to take your bags on board. But you never got that on a white-crew ship. In fact as likely as not you'd be told, ''They're your bags and you can carry them.'' On a ship with a white crew the mate was very limited in the way he could draw on his rank.'

Another contemporary and more extended contrast is offered by Jack Isbester. 'At a workaday level I find officer – crew relationships satisfactory on the British-flag ships in which I am serving. There is little acrimony, officers and ratings will generally share a few drinks in the bar or on deck at a barbecue, and individual officers will from time to time go ashore with ratings. Despite this I am conscious that, in general, officers and ratings on British ships come from different social classes and have different values. To generalise (and to think immediately of exceptions) officers still make a serious effort to protect the employers' best interests whilst ratings give the impression in their talk and in their actions that they are motivated solely by self-interest.

'I am still happier sailing with foreign crews and basically it is because I find they share my middle-class attitudes. They are ready to take us as they find us: fair treatment prompts a whole-hearted effort from most foreign seamen, and I appreciate their normal traditions of temperate behaviour, cleanliness and courtesy. Over the years I have sailed with Indians, Bangladeshis, Cape Verdes, Hondurans, Barbadians, Chinese, Zulus, Filipinos and Somalis, and I've had a lot of respect and liking for most of them.'

There is little doubt that Jack Isbester is right – that the ratings from the countries and regions he describes *are* more compliant; and that the form of loyalty to the employer found among officers is generally absent among other members of a British crew. It is normal among British ratings for them to take a strictly contractual view of their employment, although of course this does not apply in those conditions where life is at risk.

While ratings are sometimes conservative in their attitudes and politics, they generally have little love for their employers. One of the reasons for the often muted antagonisms felt towards officers is that they are too ready unquestioningly to act as the shipowners' agents. As Matt Bainbridge, himself a most conscientious seaman, puts it, 'With some of these officers, if the owners told them to put the starboard anchor down the engine-room skylight, then they'd do it. As things are now we often find ourselves at loggerheads with the owners and find the officers defending the owners even though they know that what the owners are doing is wrong. It's like a drainpipe, really. There's the owners at the top and us at the bottom and with a big clog of officers in the middle that won't let anything get through.'

In the shipping industry the employment relations for officers have been different from those for other seafarers. Officers are on a promotional ladder, and progress up it has led them to join and then stay with a company early in their career. While there have been periodic labour shortages which have disrupted the seniority system, mobility to a senior rank in another company has been unusual. The career system naturally builds in loyalty, although the necessity of 'keeping the ship moving' is a habit of mind and a way of thinking inculcated at such an early age that it becomes an automatic response. No such ways of thinking have been passed on to deck or galley boys or to young engine-room ratings. They have learned that a right-thinking seaman was a man who treasured his freedom and decided himself which ships he would sail in. For most of the post-war period the condition of the labour market and the method of finding crews ensured that seafarers could indeed pick and choose their ships and be responsible only to themselves.

Most ports had what was known as the 'Pool', an employment office run by shipowners which tried to match the requirements of ships with the availability of men. Whenever a seaman had completed a voyage and taken as much or as little leave as he

wanted and could afford, he returned to the pool. Emlyn Williams describes just how easy it was for a young AB in the mid-1970s:
'There used to be three of us shipping out together, and we could get jobs with no trouble. I remember one time we paid off the *Cotopaxi* on a Friday afternoon, stayed in Liverpool over the weekend, went down to the pool on Monday morning and were sailing out at Monday teatime. Then it was no trouble. Sometimes I'd just go home to Wales for a few days, then I'd come back, have a look around and ship out again. It was easy then, wasn't it? You could just pick and choose your ship and go where you wanted.'

Emlyn Williams went away to sea at the age of sixteen as a bridge boy on one of the last of the transatlantic liners and soon learned how easy it was to move around. 'While I was on that ship I used to hear the older lads talking about different places they'd been, and I soon decided on a change, because on that ship we only went to Montreal and Cherbourg. There were six of us bridge boys, all sharing the same cabin, and you used to see different faces all the time. We had a couple of older lads who'd been away before, and they only stayed on the *Empress* boat for a fortnight, saying that it was no good. So I was wondering what I was missing out on – so I got myself into gear and off I went.'

It is true that some men sailed regularly with one company: they were usually older hands and were known as 'company men'. There were others who had a pool contract which required them to take ships nominated by the pool in return for slightly better conditions of service. But the great majority declined either to be company men (almost a term of abuse) or to take a pool contract. With regard to the pool contract, Jim Slater's view was thoroughly typical: 'Although I was at sea for twenty-eight years, I wanted to be able to choose my ship. With a contract you couldn't do that, you were committed to whatever ship they wanted to send you to. You were tied, you were bound. Although it cost me wages and leave, it was worth it for my freedom.'

For cooks and stewards the pool system worked especially well. Even to the point where they could arrange their work on a seasonal basis, like this anonymous cook: 'I've just been on the Isle of Man boats for the summer and I've been doing this for years – and in the winter following the sun! Going off deep-sea in the winter and staying home in the summer – but it's not so easy to do that now. I didn't manage to get away last winter, and I doubt if I will this year, either. What we used to do was get on the cruises on the *Empress* boats and then come back for the Isle of Man boats. For sixteen out of the last nineteen years I've come back in the summer.'

We have seen that this ability to move around was not restricted to cooks and stewards, although seasonal variations in trades really did make it possible for them to arrange their lives as if they were rentiers. For other seamen it was more a case of deciding what part of the world they wanted to visit or whether, perhaps being newly married and needing some cash, to ship out on a tanker for a period of enforced saving. There is a trace of both these reasons in Joe Gallagher's work history:

'I did a couple of trips in the *Empress* boats [to Canada in the mid-1950s]. After that I went on PSNC boats down to South America, and then I decided I'd had enough of that and then did all the Mediterranean ports. I got fed up with that run and then went with Shell for two years – that was three ships in two years, because on those Shell tankers you tended to do long trips of about eight or nine months. After that I had a go in Esso but that was mostly round the coast ... Then I've been on Mobil and Gulf tankers.'

In practice, seamen did not move around quite as much as it might seem. Joe Gallagher, in his thirty years at sea, spent twelve of them with one company and nearly three years in just one of their ships. The point, however, was less the movement and more the possibility. No matter how illusory it was, no matter how much based on booming world trade and a still large British merchant fleet, the fact remained that seafarers could believe in their independence, that they were tied to no one and could come and go as they pleased. As one young cook forcefully put it when comparing past with present, 'There was a time when you could just tell the chief steward to go and jump over the wall, over the ship's side, and you could go to the pool and get a job. I know fellers older than me who swore blind they'd never have a contract and now they're screaming out for them.'

Now, in the changed circumstances of the 1980s, the pool is almost finished as more and more shipowners have withdrawn their financial support. Seafarers, with great reluctance, have taken company contracts in what has often turned out to be a vain attempt to get regular work.

While the main complaint made by officers about other members of the crew is what they define as 'irresponsible attitudes', the aspect of the ship's hierarchy that most angers ratings is the petty badges of status that are used to set the officers apart. These barriers and separations could produce the most bizarre relationships even within families. Emlyn Williams's uncle was a master in Ellerman's but '... only in the last few years since he retired would he talk to me much about the sea. While he was actually working he wouldn't talk to me, because he was a captain and I was an AB.'

For other seafarers it was more the symbolic things that irked most. Frank Fearon remembers: 'When I was just a kid on the cargo boats in 1965 we got blue sheets and blue pillow cases, while the officers got lovely white ones – just simple things like that. We'd get a bar of waxy soap and they'd get Lux. Their bar would always be really plush and nice with armchairs, while in ours it would be benches. If there was draught beer and only one keg left, then they'd always have it. There was no tossing up to see who'd have the last keg.'

The question of drink was always a sore point. Until recent years it was assumed that, while officers knew how to control their drinking, other members of the crew were inherently more inclined to barbarism, were deficient in self-control, and therefore needed to be rationed. This was the way Joe Gallagher saw it: 'When I was in Shell and BP the officers could get as much beer and bottles of spirits as they wanted. All *we* could have was two cans of beer a day. That's class distinction at its worst, isn't it? I've seen a young lad of an engineer or a third mate go and get a bottle of rum or whisky. I was ten years older, but the thing was that he was supposed to know better than me because he was an officer.'

The most powerful separation of officers from crew concerns the eating arrangements. Who eats with whom is, in most societies, an excellent guide to social divisions, and the ship is no exception. This very question is now a prominent one among seafarers as shipowners, anxious to save on running costs, have become social reformers as they try to introduce 'common messing'.

To see just how far this flies in the face of all normal practice and tradition we might begin with Rodney Wilson describing the situation on his first ship in the early years of World War II:

'There was a beautiful dining room there on that ship and the skipper would sit in there on his own, though sometimes he might invite the chief engineer and the mate. Standing at the door would be the chief steward at his beck and shout. The mates were in a separate messroom eating off a bare wooden table and sitting on forms, and it was the same with the engineers in their accommodation.

'The deck and down-below crowds would eat in their accommodation down aft and would come and collect their food in storm kits. There was a partition down there with a bogey stove in the middle to separate the engine-room fellers from the deck crowd.'

On cargo liners captains were generally less isolated from other officers and everyone dined in the same saloon. Even then, however, it was still common in the late 1950s for mates and engineers to dine at separate tables. Here, for example, is Roger O'Hara describing the saloon seating arrangements on the Blue Funnel ship *Adrastus*:

'In the saloon there were two main tables, and when there were no passengers one would be taken up by the captain and officers and the other would be for the chief and the engineers. Mates and engineers would never sit down together. I've never seen that. It wouldn't happen and you wouldn't even *think* of it. And then on each table you all had your own seat where you *always* sat, because where you sat was a matter of seniority: you sat in order of your rank. With the mates you'd just never get to know them. You'd never know their names, even. You'd call them Third Mate, Second Mate, and so on.'

Even more formalised segregations applied among the crew. Here is Tony Santamara describing the crew's arrangements: 'Six years ago I was on a ferry that had twenty-eight NUS members in the crew and there were the three usual departments – deck, engine room, catering – but there were four messrooms. The ABs' mess, the stewards' mess, the down-below mess, the POs' mess. But *we* didn't design that, it was the shipowners. They didn't ask us what we wanted. They wanted to divide us up. And so what happened was that departments would vie with each other. The POs would be sitting in their mess, talking about their aspect of shipboard politics; the ABs would be talking about the bosun; the down-below fellers would be talking about the store-keeper, and they'd *all* be complaining about the catering department! Now from a commonsense point of view and sitting down and thinking about building a ship and with a crew of only twenty-eight – well, you'd have to have a good reason for building the ship with four messrooms, wouldn't you?'

Perhaps a more likely explanation of the absurdity just reported is that the naval architects who designed the ship were advised by marine superintendents who were ex-masters and ex-chief engineers. Such people without even thinking about it would enshrine in steel bulkheads their views as to the proper hierarchy of the ship. This is certainly credible, for among ratings, too, there is a tendency to unthinkingly absorb and accept the pettiest discriminations. A classic example is Tony Santamara's 'orange juice incident':

'In looking at this class thing you even have to take into account things like menus. Let me tell you this story of what happened on a Townsend Thoreson ferry out of Felixstowe in 1974. I was an assistant steward on there, and one morning I was having this glass of orange juice for my breakfast and I saw the second steward go past and look into the messroom. I knew from the way he looked that something was going to be up, so I went down by his cabin to listen to what he was going to say. I heard him talking to the barman and the storekeeper: "Did you see that bloody Santamara down there drinking orange juice in the mess-room?" Hearing that, I walked in and asked what it had to do with him if I was drinking orange juice, and had he bought it himself? He said that I could have all the orange juice I wanted but would I mind not drinking it in the messroom because otherwise they would all want it and they weren't supposed to have it. I said that the officers had it and why shouldn't everyone else?

'I got very bolshie about it, but, the way it turned out, it had nothing to do with the company, because they assumed that *everybody* was getting orange juice. What it was, was this second steward hanging on to what he'd learned in other ships about what it was proper for officers to have, and he'd assumed that the crew didn't get orange juice. I had another run in with the same feller about giving salmon paste to an AB!'

Disputes of this sort had their origins in the long history of providing officers with better and more varied food. In the early years of this century it was normal for a shipowner to spend twice as much on provisions for officers as for other members of the crew. By the 1970s the gap had almost disappeared but chief stewards might find it hard to adjust to this egalitarian intrusion and insist on maintaining superficial differences. Joe Taylor recalls that in Elders & Fyffes:

'The captain and officers had breakfast, lunch and dinner while the crew had breakfast, dinner and tea. This was class distinction, I would say, because the food wasn't any different. The officers would have the usual breakfast of bacon, egg and black pud; for lunch they'd have a mixed grill, and roast lamb for dinner. The crew would have the same breakfast but they'd have the lamb for their dinner at midday and the mixed grill for tea in the evening.'

The issue on ships today is not about the names attached to different meals, nor is it about differences in quality of food as between mess and saloon – it is about whether officers and crew should take their food together in the same room. The question arouses strong passions among officers, many of whom see dining off white linen and being waited upon by white-jacketed stewards as an essential part of their status. Chris Warlow says of this: 'One of the things that attracts you to sea in the first place is what you see in the shiny brochures, and if you see a smartly dressed steward in his white jacket then that's been part of the attraction.' There were similar remarks from Andrew Milligan: 'I suppose one of the perks of being an officer has been getting silver service, and I must say I wouldn't like to see that going.'

This concern for maintaining the 'civilised' style of the smart restaurant in the saloon can often be a cover for an unspoken comparison with the relative 'barbarism' of the mess. As one senior officer said, 'I still feel that the officer has to be segregated from the crew; he most certainly must be. I don't expect the master to be sitting down with some AB who's slovenly and whose eating habits are disgusting, and neither would I expect the chief engineer to do the same thing either.' Another senior officer, having said that he did not get 'steamed up' about common messing and was willing to give it a try, later went to the trouble of writing a retraction from his ship in Australasia:

'Having sailed from the Persian Gulf to New Zealand and after spending two weeks in a New Zealand port with the present crew, under no circumstances would I advocate the integration of messing facilities on board ships of the British Merchant Navy. I can see now that it would be an impossible task, considering the social behaviour of the majority of ratings on this ship. I find it almost intolerable to be on the same ship. I balk at the idea of having to spend my off-duty hours with them.'

Hearing and understanding the judgements made about them, including those which are unspoken or coded, there is among other crew members a huge lake of resentment. Sometimes, in splurges of excess, it seems as if those who are despised take an embittered and perverse delight in acting out the part which the officers' stereotype requires from them. The tacit claims made by officers to superior personal qualities are bound to be provocative when the wider society bases its claim to moral superiority on the ground of its democratic practice. The sense of outrage frequently felt by seafarers is pungently expressed here by Bernie McNamee:

'They're no better than I am and I'm no better than them but they still think they're a better class. That's a load of nonsense. They're just the same as us and they get drunk just the same as we do. If you're out there at sea and one man's in the water – if it's the skipper or the mate, and you hate him, and he falls overboard, the first thing you do is get in after him. Now if that's what it is, then why the hell can't we mess together? That's my attitude!'

These sentiments of egalitarianism strike very deep, and to those who cleave to them as staunchly as Bernie McNamee claims to superior worth excite anger, derision and contempt.

In acknowledgement of the spread of democratic sentiment and practice it is now common for officers to use first names with other members of the crew – and so it does seem as if there is some ambivalence and ambiguity among officers. Mick Gibbons catches some of this: 'These days we're on a first-name basis, but there was none of that during the war. It was in-your-place sort of thing and no cameraderie. Now it's a lot better, though whether or not they mean it I don't know. I think a lot of them do mean it, the decent ones. There are some who still think they're better than you. It's the "I've served my time" sort of thing and "I didn't do this for nothing".'

A ship's cook makes a similar point when he compares two captains with whom he has recently sailed. 'One just treats you as a fellow human being but in some ways goes so far as to put you on a higher level. I mean, he'll recognise that as a cook, for example, you know more than he does, and he'll defer to you. He might call you by your first name but I'll always call him "Captain". Let's put it this way: the man's a lot older than me, and he's earned the title of being called Captain because he's a good one. Give credit where it's due is my policy.'

For the other captain there are strong words and stronger feelings. 'This guy is filth. He disgusts me every time I look at him – that's how bad he is. How can I explain him? He speaks as if he's got a plum in his mouth, as if got his accent from Harrod's. It's his attitude to life. When he's on the bridge he wears one of these baseball caps. And then there's his sunglasses, his epaulettes on his sweater; there's scrambled egg and gold braid all over him. There's more scrambled egg on him than there is in the galley. And then he comes out with "Morning, Second Cook – and what have we got for breakfast?" in that posh voice of his. I just ignore him. He's not there for me.'

Few officers attract either so much approval as the former or so much outrage as the latter. Although it is normal, as much elsewhere as aboard ship, for judgements about persons to be separated from judgements made about them as members of a class or group, it is rarely possible for people to step far enough outside the group to be seen only as an individual. This is especially true of the closed hierarchical community of the ship.

The judgements that have been voiced about officers and by officers have come at a time when what might be called *traditional* ways of exercising authority have been challenged in most corners of society where the classes meet face-to-face. Here, we have seen one of the responses to that challenge in the use by officers of first names when addressing other crew members. This practice came as a profound shock to Dave Kirkwood after twelve years in the Royal Navy:

'To me, the Merchant Navy officers seemed to be completely different in their attitudes and the way they spoke to you. It was all first names. In the Navy they'd call me by my surname or 'You, lad,' while in the Merchant Navy I've found the mate invite me down to his cabin for a can after the watch. I couldn't comprehend this at first. I was wondering what he was after, but what I've found is that they're just trying to be friendly. They've found out – as we've found out – that we're the same people.'

This mutual discovery, however, is rather fragile, for in another context Dave Kirkwood says that some deck officers would like to '... treat you like a rating in the RN' and that officers are commonly referred to as the 'pigs'. These suspicions are connected with an acceptance of a hierarchy based on skill. To quote Dave Kirkwood again, 'The thing is, you've got to have some form of thing where someone is leader. It's all very well us taking the mickey out of them but, when all's said and done, they're getting paid to be leaders, even though some of them couldn't show you the way to the nearest toilet.' The same kind of rationale is also used by crew members when they express *their* reservations about common messing. Tony Hinks, for example, expresses a widely held view that bosses and workers are best kept apart:

'I might have a set-to with the second engineer. Nothing vicious, but cross words, so we don't talk, we just go about our daily business ignoring each other. Now if we're sitting down to eat with each other that's a bit difficult. You see, you've still got to have that situation where he's the boss. If you're drinking and eating with a chap, then things might get too familiar and make it difficult for me to accept him as a boss and hard for him to give me a rollicking.'

In an extension of the same argument Matt Bainbridge says, 'I've never known a ship's captain put his head on the block to save mine, and I doubt that I'll ever live long enough to see it! On the ship I'm on now the Old Man asked me what I thought about communal messing and I told him I was against. 'Why?' he asked. 'We all get along all right.' But my attitude is that it's all right being very nice to these people until the shit hits the fan – and then it goes back to how it was before: very sharpish.'

The issue of who eats with whom does raise fundamental questions about the fabric of convictions and conventions that sustain the shipboard hierarchy, and that is why people of *all* ranks are made so uneasy by it. Stripped to its essentials, the object of hierarchy is to ensure that the officers are able to subordinate the crew to the interests of the shipowner. Both legally and in fact, the master is the shipowner's agent and the other officers are simply an extension of the master's authority. The Merchant Shipping Acts give the master wide-ranging powers:

The Master of any ship registered in the United Kingdom may cause any person on board the ship to be put under restraint of and for so long as it appears to him necessary or expedient in the interest of safety or for the preservation of good order or discipline on board the ship.[9]

These legal powers have become wrapped and overlaid with customs, conventions and contrivances which 'sanctify' legal authority by presenting its agent as superior persons well fitted by certification and personal quality.

The authority of certification is usually unquestioned. When Peter Carney says forgivingly of junior engineers who are a bit cocky with their new uniforms and one stripe, 'I suppose that's understandable, they've put in a long time at college, haven't they?' he is reaffirming the belief that authority based on skill is justified. What promotes the unease raised by the issue of common messing is how the exercise of authority will be affected by the *social* equality implied in taking food together. It is the prospect of social and personal egalitarianism that produces so much anxiety among officers, and that is why it is they, not the ratings, who are vocal and organised in their opposition to common messing. For their part, other crew members think it might be difficult to enjoy the normal messroom pastime of complaining and joking about officers. Implicit in this is the view that common messing is a threat to crew solidarity. The objections voiced by Matt Bainbridge and heard from many others run parallel. They are concerned that the conflicts of interest between shipowners and seafarers might be masked if social relationships between officers and crew became too close, and effective trade unionism therefore blunted. That, of course, is a possibility. Another one is that seafarers' trade unionism in general might become more effective through greater unity.

II

Thus far this chapter has been concerned mainly with the divisions between officers and crew, and the emphasis is justified because of their pervasiveness and recent public topicality. In the daily life of the ship there are other divisions which have their own momentum and impact and which were mentioned previously. These concern the evaluations placed upon different kinds of work, and a good insight into these is provided by Tony Santamara:

'ABs have this sort of macho thing with them: up the rigging and down the mast, over the side on stages, and that sort of thing. For them the stewards are all queers; particularly years ago, you used to get a lot of that. But with the ABs it's different according to the type of ship.

'I was on a Blue Star boat in 1968, and the ABs there used to work all the hours and they regarded themselves as some sort of glamour boys, going ashore in New Zealand with their well washed Wranglers, and some of them loved stalking around the deck with their belts and sheath knives. The stewards would have less bronzie than the ABs; they'd look more on the pale side. I often used to say that if the AB had to do his bronzie in his own time he'd be the whitest man on the ship.

'Now all that's on cargo boats, but on the passenger boats the catering staff were the boys, because they were where the money was. They generally ran all the rackets. They ran the gambling, they were the wheelers and dealers, they could get off with the women because they were with the passengers. On these ships things were switched around, whereas on the cargo boats, unless you were a particularly handsome cook or steward and well bronzied, you didn't stand much chance in New Zealand or Australia. In fact I remember stewards dressing to look like ABs.'

Ideas of 'men's' work and 'women's' work have been a continuing source of conflict among crews, and inevitably, given the division of labour in most households, the work of cooks and stewards has been regarded as 'woman's work'. And then, as if to complicate matters, in some of the passenger trades there were seagoing communities of homosexuals and transvestites, and they consisted mainly of catering staff. The Royal Mail Line ships trading to Latin America and the Orient Line trading to Australia and the Far East were especially well known as almost the only places where males who were not heterosexual dared to be open about themselves. The inferior status of catering work was also 'confirmed' by the fact that since the days of sail the only shipboard job that was commonly done by black seafarers was the cook's. It was still the same in the 1950s, for, as Hermon McKay says, 'In Lamport's they'd only allow colour in the galley. Now there's a contradiction! You don't like black fellers but you don't mind having him do your food!'

Mates and engineers could generally be relied upon to subscribe just as keenly as the ABs to the cult of the male, and so it is only to be expected that among cooks and stewards are heard the strongest reactions to the social pretensions of officers. As Tony Santamara says, 'Amongst the crews you do find different degrees of resentment about class distinction, and I think you'll find that stewards tend to resent it most, because they experience it the most. They have to clean the officers' toilets, make their beds, clean their rooms, wait on them at table.'

As so often in these circumstances, underdogs find their own ways of getting even. A cook talks of the sorts of ruses that could be used against arrogant officers: 'One of the things we used to do was put plate powder in the soup – you know, that powder you used to use for cleaning the silver. You could put a few drops of that in the soup. Another thing was putting a few 'Jasper's' eggs in their suitcases before paying off. When they got home they'd put their suitcases on the top of the wardrobe and after a time the house would be flooded out with cockroaches.'

ABs still tend to think of themselves, along with the mates, as the only 'proper seamen'. It is they who are out in the elements; out under the sky and face to face with the sea. Up on the bridge, keeping a look-out or perhaps even steering from time to time, it is easy to forget how critically dependent they are upon those who work in the engine room. So powerful are the folk legends of seafaring as a struggle against nature and so remindful of the legends are the sounds and visual effects of a storm that mates and ABs can fall into the romantic illusion that they alone are the true sailors. Cooks and stewards, by contrast, do no such manly things and, although the officers and motormen in the engine room plainly do 'men's' work, it cannot be described as sailoring. These sentiments are shared by ABs and mates alike, and that is why Billy Kerrigan could say that 'Even in the harder ships you'll find there's a bit of comradeship between the mates and the crowd.'

Each of the shipboard departments nourishes its own solidarities between officers and ratings. In each case it is not just face-to-face working that binds – there are also sets of ideas that they have of themselves. Among cooks and stewards on the passenger ships there is their unrivalled access to desirable goods and activities which persuades them of their ascendency and enables them to see themselves as the fixers and the organisers. In the deck department we have already seen the potency of the ideas about man and nature. Among engineers and motormen there is a well justified pride in their resourcefulness, in their readiness and ability to take on major jobs which in a shore establishment would call for specialist contractors.

If in each *department* the resentments of hierarchy are smoothed and modified, there are also ways in which seafarers are brought together so that everyone from the master to the galley boy is self-consciously a member of the community of the sea. There is more than a hint of this in the following story, told by Captain Jack Tanner, a story which can plainly be read as a salute to the superior strength and determination of merchant seamen:

'I remember once in Cyprus a British army major came to see me at seven-thirty in the morning to tell me that there'd been a bit of trouble ashore the previous evening – that my crew and some of his lads had been involved in a fight in a bar. I asked him how many had been involved and he said there must have been quite a few, because there were twenty-two of his.

'I sent for the bosun and he came up with a terrific eye, it was one of the worst eyes I've ever seen. The army officer was still there, and I asked the bosun what had happened and he said he'd been involved in a fight with some squaddies. I asked him who was involved and how many and he said it was only himself and three ABs. The major couldn't believe this. He said, surely there must have been many more? The bosun insisted that there'd only been the four of them and if the squaddies hadn't started kicking with their boots they'd have "murdered" them!'

Everyone in this community knows that, layered and divided as they are, their way of living sets them apart. As Len Holder puts it, 'I think this battle with the elements, so to speak, tends to breed a degree of conformity and a sort of common interest or group spirit.' One of the consequences is that even after the most extreme antagonisms there can be an overarching sense of unity. This is exceptionally well illustrated by an incident early in Hermon McKay's career at sea. It was in Bahia Blanca, Argentina, in 1947 and he was a seventeen-year-old cabin boy. He had bought a bottle of wine to take home as a present but was stopped at the top of the gangway by the mate and told that he couldn't bring drink aboard. An argument ensued and the mate got thumped. The upshot for Hermon was two days in the local calaboose and a fine the equivalent of two months' pay. By the end of the voyage he was due to pay off with 9s 6d after almost nine months away. At the pay-off in Belfast his shipmates had a whip-round for him, and then something else happened which left him speechless:

'I was a bit embarrassed and didn't know how to handle it. You see, the mate that I had this run-in with came up to me and gave me £10. He just gave it to me and then walked away. I was tongue-tied and didn't know what to say. There was none of this 'Here you are and just go away and behave yourself', he just gave it to me and disappeared. That was when I began to understand things; that was when I was becoming a man. You see, despite the divisions on the ship between the officers and the crew, they're not really that much. There is that brotherhood too.'

And yet just a few sentences later, he says: 'The way I read it is that officers are brought up to regard you as scum. If they want to claw their way up to being skippers or chief engineer and to reach the dizzy heights they've got to treat us as scum. Some of them relish it but there's others, obviously, who maintain a distance between you but won't treat you like scum.'

The apparent contradiction is, of course, nothing of the kind. There is the knowledge that the experience of hierarchy will vary with the disposition and social outlook of senior officers, and that antagonisms may always be modified by the solidarity of seafaring. What is generally apparent, especially for ABs, cooks, stewards and motormen, is that the system is puzzling. There is, therefore, an inconclusiveness as to a clear line on the subject of hierarchy. People reach for an embracing generalisation which is firm, clear and simple. And then modify it or withdraw it. For all the bitternesses and all the fears there are also the ambivalences, the ambiguities, the alliances, and it is these that save the isolated community of the ship from social warfare.

Notes

1   Humfrey Jordan, *Sea Way Only*, London, 1937, pp. 11–12.
2   'Taffrail', *Blue Star Line*, London, 1948, p. 12.
3   For P&O see: P. Padfield, *Beneath the House Flag of the P&O*,

London, 1981; for Royal Mail see: R. Woolward, *Nigh on Sixty Years at Sea*, London, 1894.

4   Geoffrey Dowd's *Whiffs From the Briny*, London, 1931, Pt. 3, is one of the many accounts of RNR training which are unintended caricatures.

5   H.W. Edwards. *Under Four Flags*, London, 1954, pp.156–7.

6   For an exploration of this process see my 'Neither officers nor gentlemen', *History Workshop Journal*, No. 19, spring 1985.

7   D.G.O. Baillie, *A Sea Affair*, London, 1957, p.173.

8   *Ibid.*, p.195.

9   J.S. Kitchen, *The Employment of Merchant Seamen*, London, 1980, p.48.

[VII] · *Concluding*

Ah! These commercial interests –
spoiling the finest life under the sun.
Why must the sea be used for trade … ? – *Joseph Conrad*

Seafarers have responded to the sudden and calamitous decline of merchant shipping with a mood that oscillates between anger and disbelief. News items from the Merchant Navy Programme, broadcast on the BBC's World Service, might trigger incredulous debates in saloon and messroom. Articles in *The Seaman* and *The Telegraph*, the journals respectively of the ratings' and officers' unions, might provoke sputterings of anger as the latest news is more redundancies and more companies selling ships and flagging out. In the welter of news about shipping it sometimes seems as if seafarers are drunk on data.

Shipping has for long been the most international of industries, and one of the consequences is an astonishing flow of high-quality information, most of it in the English language. A periodical literature produces data, commentary and analysis of all aspects of ship operation, and the unique daily shipping press disseminates this and other intelligence very rapidly. The range, depth and quality of information are reflected in the union journals, which are among the best to be found anywhere.

Despite the abundance of information, only handfuls of seafarers have had the education and experience to create order and understanding out of the ceaseless flow of facts. The training and education provides for seafarers, reflecting the technical and functional requirements of shipowners, have never so much as been lightly brushed by the philosophy of a liberal education. The basic and obligatory syllabuses have never required even a basic grounding in the economics and politics of world shipping.

The news and knowledge that seafarers receive of shipping developments are, for the most part, news of the consequences of decisions previously made by shipowners and operators. While seafarers know very well about the impact these decisions may have on them, they know very little about *how* the decisions have been made. They know so little of the inhabitants, the ground rules and the thought processes of the world of the ship operator that almost everything to do with them is abstract and 'out there'. The work of seafaring has been so 'designed' and organised as to exclude receiving and acting upon the sort of intelligence which is picked over by ship operators as a matter of daily routine. The business of seafaring is not the same as the business of shipping, and the existence of two separate and distinct divisions of labour has enormous consequences for the way seafarers think and act upon their place in the world.

Deprived of the tools of analysis, seafarers are understandably apt to be uncertain and sometimes confused. Emlyn Williams's response, therefore, is quite a typical one: 'I don't really know how I feel about what is happening to shipping, because I'm not sure what has caused it. If I really knew the ins and outs of it I might feel a bit bitter but I'm not too sure, really, so I don't know who to be angry at.'

Older hands might be able to draw on extensive experience, and so they quarry their memories in search of clues and ponder on the significance of those they find. Captain Fred Patten, for instance, wonders if the Ellerman management might not have had a 'death wish', so adept was it at building beautiful but inefficient ships: 'When I first joined Ellerman's in 1950 we had a class of four or five ships which were scaled-down City boats. They had turbines and were very expensive to run because in the Mediterranean you spent a lot of time at anchor, and keeping steam on the boilers so that you were ready to move at a moment's notice meant you had to use as much fuel in a day at anchor as you would in a motor ship at sea and steaming. On top of that, they had to carry 250 tons of steel in their bottom as permanent ballast because they were unstable. We also had another class of five ships known as the market boats. They were twin-screw and beautiful little ships but very poor cargo carriers and they carried 100 tons of granite in the bottom of No. 2 hatch because they were also unstable.'

A senior officer in the same firm was scathing about shore management's fads, foibles and fashions that seemed to come in recurrent waves as the company's economic plight steadily worsened in the 1970s: 'The most incredible things happened. We used to go to these meetings for a get-together at Marlow, where we'd discuss management in general and the company and that sort of thing. At one point the company got hold of some Danish consultants and they brought out some fancy system where everything was to be costed and budgeted for aboard ship. And then the whole thing was packed in and something else was tried which also got scrapped. All these systems came to naught in the end, but they must have spent thousands and thousands on them.'

Among those who sailed with family-owned or controlled firms decline is often thought to be the result of the displacement of family by professional managers. Captain George Hardy provides a model example of this theme. Saddened by the run-down of Blue Funnel, he refuses to believe that it was inevitable: 'I think Blue Funnel started going down the nick when the family were no longer involved. Until about seventeen years ago there was still a Holt there; that was George. But Lawrence Holt, of course, was a very strong character. The sea staff used to think he was marvellous. That was because he thought we were marvellous and that the shore staff were only there to support us. His attitude was that sea staff came first. In most companies it used to be the other way round .... I don't really know how to put it ... there have been too many whizz kids taken into management and who've known very little about ships – and no feeling for ships and the sea.'

There are many different ways of adjusting to decline, and resort to explanations critical of company organisation and practice is extremely common among officers as they pick over the bones and entrails. Officers may defend shore managements to the crew but, talking among themselves, the opinions can be vigorous and vitriolic.

Another and more subtle mode of adjustment involves discounting and denying the present as a time in which it is possible to be a 'proper seafarer'. The two passages which follow, from a master and a chief engineer respectively, provide excellent examples of this method of 'escape'. The master says, 'When I was deep-sea ships were run by shipowners and now they're run by accountants. The shipowners had a pride in their ships' looking nice but I don't suppose the accountants ever see the damn ship. They're not interested in whether it's nicely painted, and then once the owners' standards go down so do those of the people on the ship, because they can't have the same pride. You used to make sure that when the ship was coming into the home port it was immaculate. Now you see ships coming in which look a real bloody mess. Sometimes you get the ship managers or whatever they call themselves blaming the crew for the state of the ship when it's not their fault, it's forced on them.'

In the following remarks from a chief engineer the view which says, 'Why mourn the loss of ships when the game has changed so much anyway?' is much more explicit:

'Until 1979 I'd been in and out of the Caribbean for twelve years. If I was on the container ship, the *Astronomer*, I was hitting Jamaica nine times a year and I was going to Barbados six or seven times a year. If my wife was asked where I was going she would say I was off to Barbados as if I was getting into the car to go off down to Ormskirk – and in fact it was the same. It was seven or eight days from Liverpool to Barbados. We were getting into the tropics almost before I'd got my bag unpacked. After ten years or so of going to the Caribbean and the Mexican Gulf it was just like a shuttle service. It didn't do anything for me at all, especially after containerisation.

'Every time you wake up you're in a different port. It's just a bus service. There's no character to these ships today like in days gone by where you sat in port for ten days, did a day's work and then up the road in the evening to enjoy yourself, to sample the sights. On the container ship you might have six to twelve hours in Kingston or Barbados and you wouldn't have time to go up the road because there was always something to be done and you hadn't the manpower to take time off. *On those ships it's not really like being at sea.* [Emphasis added.]

'One of the things that started to disillusion me with my life at sea was that with all this technology I wasn't enjoying myself so much. I like to go abroad and see different things and enjoy different parts of the world but today you can't do that. And as for tankers and chemical carriers, their berths are always miles and miles away from anywhere. The young men at sea today don't enjoy themselves. I think they just check on how much money's going into the bank, but when I was younger I wasn't concerned with that.'

The experience of being made redundant and the acute anxiety about the future for those who remain also involves an unfavourable comparison between past and present. The treatment experienced by one ex-Ellerman master obviously came as an enormous shock and was hard to reconcile with his understanding of the relationship between himself and his firm. When asked how he had felt when he stepped off the gangway of his last ship, he said:

'Well, I didn't know then that that was what I was doing. I was home on leave and I had a 'phone call to go to the Shipping Federation doctor for a medical. At that time I'd been with Ellerman's for over thirty-three years and I'd never had a single medical. Now the thing was that if you were medically unfit your redundancy payment was only £1,000!

'I passed the medical, and then four or five days later I got a 'phone call asking me to go down to London, and of course I knew what it was about. I felt pretty sick. I'd been with Ellerman's for over thirty-three years, and *you* can't just forget thirty-three years like *they* can. It wasn't the thought that I might not have another ship that worried me. It was the way I was being treated. They'd asked for loyalty and they'd got it, and then, just like that, they didn't want it any more.'

In a much younger master who still had a ship there was nevertheless that same sense of fractured loyalty, of betrayal. There is a saddened, puzzled bitterness as he looks out over the foredeck of his ship that is nearing the end of its life and could at any time be sent on its last voyage to the breakers: 'When I came back to sea after a spell ashore, the British merchant fleet was short of officers, and that was only seven years ago. What has happened since wouldn't have seemed possible then. You almost feel as if you've been conned, because there were all those adverts trying to encourage people back to sea. You almost feel as if you've been used. Here you are, they've got you back, and then seven years later ...'

Officers were particularly likely to find the decline of the shipping industry hard to cope with. The very idea of officer status and progression through a career presupposed a commitment to one employer who was in turn securely lodged in a stable and orderly world. But when the world is disrupted and then threatens to fall apart the whole basis of understanding one's role in it also begins to collapse.

The sense of shock is most prevalent among the older and more senior officers who have, quite naturally, become most accustomed to the idea of an orderly world. Their younger colleagues are more worldly, invest little capital in loyalty and concentrate on survival. A young engineer described the situation as being one where people keep their heads down for fear of the brown envelope:

'Every day you're living under the threat of the big brown envelope. The way it is now in our company and where a lot of other companies are concerned is that 'If you don't like it, lump it, and if you want to make a complaint, go away'. It's got to the point where people such as mates and seconds want to keep a low profile. They don't want to bring themselves to the company's attention because they might get the brown envelope. They don't want to spend; they won't order this and they won't order that. Ships are getting tatty, and they won't kick up to keep the ship in the pristine condition it should be kept in. I've sailed on ships twenty-five years old that were in pristine condition, they were beautifully kept. Now you can go on a ship that's only two or three years old and it looks like a tub. But no one wants to make any waves, no one wants to kick up. They just want to keep a nice low profile so they don't get that big brown envelope with the redundancy notice in it and join the 3·5 million unemployed.'

There is no doubt that fear and uncertainty produce compliance, although in that respect shipowners never had any problems with their officers. But, in these new conditions, officers feel that between them and their employers there is now less mutual respect and more coercion. Relations are certainly not improved when employers succumb to the familiar British managerial disease of deflecting criticism of themselves on to their workers. In this connection Dario Vieceli says:

'One thing that upsets people at sea is that on any job we're always being told that the Germans or the Danes or the Norwegians can do it cheaper than us, only to find that their running costs must be higher than ours even though their charter costs are lower. In other words, they must be getting a subsidy to run the ship. With some of these ships they have exactly the same size crew as us and everyone knows they're better paid. What upsets us as well is that while British owners are chartering in these ships and selling their own, what will happen when things do pick up again? We'll just be left high and dry with no ships and no jobs. The British shipowners just aren't making any provision for the future, and the way we're going on I really don't think there will be a British merchant navy left. It's frightening now – and nobody wants to know.'

John Goble, who has seen two-thirds of the Palm Line fleet disappear from around him since 1977, has armoured himself with a well cultivated fatalism. Like Dario Vieceli he too believes that 'nobody wants to know' and has been steadily preparing himself for the worst:

'So far as politicians are concerned there's no electoral mileage in the shipping industry. I don't think the great mass of people in this country are even aware that we have a shipping industry. They either think we've got a huge one because they know someone who was in Cunard thirty years ago, or they live in Peterborough, have never known anyone who has gone to sea and probably think exports float out of Britain of their own accord. For all that we're a maritime nation there's no one who really seems to want to support the shipping industry.

'I've had the idea for some years now that the shipping industry wasn't going to last my working lifetime. In the late '70s I'd seen both Denholm's and Harrison's going down. From a point in the early and mid-'70s where they couldn't get enough men to sail their ships they were now at a point where it seemed they couldn't sell ships fast enough. It's hard to remember now that in 1974 it was all boom, boom, boom – and then suddenly the bottom went out of the bulk shipping market and containerisation was spreading to more and more of the liner trades. By the late '70s it was obvious that people like Yugoslavs and Filipinos would be crewing the ships of the future.

'Shipping is a "low tech." industry. It's like the textile industry, isn't it? It's no longer the preserve of the advanced countries, it's become the preserve of the second-rank nations – Singapore, Taiwan, the Philippines – these are the shipping nations of the future. This is progress, isn't it? You can't fight against it. Well, perhaps progress isn't quite the right word, it's just change, isn't it?'

John Goble may well be broadly right in his assessment of trends in world shipping, and there is certainly no doubt that seafarers, regardless of age, experience and rank, feel themselves to be in the grip of immutable forces that 'you can't fight against'. Faced with the sheer scale and pace of change, Hermon McKay thinks everyone is 'punch drunk': 'When they see that the likes of Harrison's have gone, that Blue Funnel has gone. These were our landmarks. They were part of the world. They *were* our world and they've gone.'

These observations are profounder than the face-value words

reveal, and although Hermon McKay is reporting the sense of loss felt by people like himself – that is to say, motormen, ABs, cooks and stewards – there is a close and obvious connection with what we have heard from officers. We should expect this from those who grew up with shipping and the shipping communities of the big ports where learning to recognise ships, to know where they went and what cargoes they brought back was all a central part of early learning. By knowing these things they were knowing their futures as certainly as country boys learning to recognise the change of season by the texture of light and the feel on the face of the morning air. Different ships, that is to say, became as much a part of the mental map of the landscape as a river or a mountain and with the same apparent quality of being fixed in time and space. Ships, it is true, might go to the breakers, but others were as certainly launched to take their place.

This apparent permanency of ships and shipping was an unavoidable sentiment for the John Dooligans and the John Gobles who knew the funnels; it was not very much different for all the others who went away to sea in their mid-'teens and subsequently knew little of any other way of life. We have seen in an earlier chapter the importance of recognising silhouettes and colour schemes, and how just to use the words 'Harrison's' and 'Blue Funnel' could release an avalanche of images and an oral encyclopaedia of all the information a seafarer could want to know. Imagine, therefore, the disorientation that must follow when parts of the landscape disappear, when 'Harrison's' and 'Blue Funnel' are names that have only a past. And because they offer a past that had some stability, which compares favourably with a present which has only uncertainty, the past itself begins to gleam with the polish of nostalgia and be a better place to 'live' in.

The world of ships that has been lost to so many of the present generations of seafarers has also been lost to those who might have been their successors. This is a loss that Hermon McKay feels very sharply. 'The opportunities for young people to go away to sea for a while to see a bit of the world, those have gone for ever. You know, for all the bad things that have happened in the past there was one door open for black youth – the sea. It broadened your horizons. It broke down the ghetto mentality. It was an education for you. It was the last card in the deck, but it was something that you could be a galley boy, a trimmer, even a deck boy. But what have they got here, the youth? They've got a ghetto mentality. They can't see any way out, and it makes them anti-*everything*. For us there was an escape, there was a loophole. This is where I feel for them. Looking back on what I got out of it, I can see what they're missing.'

Almost every single one of the seafarers who appear in this book found his or her way into seafaring careers through members or friends or connections of their families. The existing 'community' of seafarers recruited the next generation; they 'spoke' for them, wrote references for them, made contacts for them. But this, the current generation of seafarers, finds itself with only the shadow of a network to tap into and hardly any contacts to use to assist the passage of *their* young into the adult world. The world that has been lost is not just a personal loss, private to the individual seafarer, it is a loss to a coming generation.

One of the recurring emphases of this book has been on the importance to seafarers of their understanding of what being 'a proper seafarer' involves. What is conspicuously *not* present in this self-definition is any sense of being immersed in a commercial enterprise in a way that a banker would recognise. The demands of commerce that come into this life are felt as necessary but alien intrusions.

It is not the carriage of the objects of commerce that intrudes. On the contrary, this part of ship activity is often a source of pride, because shifting goods that people need helps sustain a sense of being of service that is untouched by motives of personal gain. These sentiments of *service* run very strongly indeed among merchant seafarers, which is why they prefer terms like 'merchant navy', 'merchant service' and 'mercantile marine' to the more worldly and accurate 'shipping industry'.

Commerce and 'the company', which is hidden from seafarers by the ignorance imposed upon them, do nevertheless become revealed, albeit in a limited and restricted way. The company shows itself as the author of restrictions, of sanctions, of permissions and refusals. 'The company' is something that ominously and anonymously stands over and outside the community of seafarers. Company functionnaries are seen as 'meddling clerks' who are ignorant of the sea and ships; they are accountants who have sold their souls to columns of figures and who know nothing of the *man's* life at sea. These attitudes are soon acquired and widely shared across generation and rank as they join in their solidarity of contempt for the 'office'. Such attitudes, however, are essentially defensive.

The fact is that seafarers are afraid of the shore and only confident of themselves when aboard ship or in the company of other seafarers. Many years ago William McFee wrote of a group of engineers going back to their ship in the early morning, 'We had a subconscious urge to get back to the ship. We felt safer there than anywhere else. Emotionally safer, that is. The ship was our home, our way of life, our conception of security. We hurried towards it.'[1] 'The company', which was the most threatening embodiment of the shore was, by contrast, something to be avoided. It was and still is a commonplace that captains might be like lions aboard their ships and as mice when confronted with an officious chief clerk: at home in the world of seafaring and hopelessly out of depth in the world of shipping.

Further reinforcement for the separate role of seafaring has come from the powerful legends of the part played in wartime by the shipping industry and its translation by royal adoption into the Merchant Navy. The rhetoric of service facilitated by the very large loss of life in two world wars, and recently revived by the Falklands adventure, causes an immense amount of confusion. It so encourages seafarers to believe that they are employed in a service, that they are unable to contend with the real world of shipping that is propelled by different imperatives.

Seafarers are caught in the trap of preferring to believe that the world *is* what they think it *ought* to be. On this question, at least, seafarers are as near one mind as they will ever be. Meanwhile the younger, more skilled and resourceful redundant seafarers have made other lives for themselves. Those who have lived seafaring the longest and will never know any other employment find it hard to accept that the world that was their life has gone ...

Once or twice a week Barney Moussa was dropping in to the International Seafarers' Centre on Liverpool waterfront.[2] There were always other men there who, like him, could not quite believe how quiet the Mersey was and that they could not now go into the Pool over the road and come out with the name of a ship and a joining time:

'I'm sixty but I'm still very young and I'm very experienced as a seaman, because I've never done anything else except pull on rope and clean the boiler. I don't know anything about electrical work, about fitting, about plumbing, about bricklaying, about anything else. All I know? Paint the ship's side and make a cup of tea for the officers.

'When the men come ashore they're waiting here now, just like us. They're waiting for the ships, but there aren't any ships. We just sit down; we're lost, we don't know where to go now. We'll sit here watching the Shipping Federation [the Pool] but there's nothing coming out of there. We look at the time – and then go to the bar and drink it. We go home. We come here again tomorrow and they say to you, ''No job for you.'' '

References

1 W. McFee, *In the First Watch*, London, 1947, p. 56.
2 Even this, the last refuge, has now closed.

APPENDIX

The diagrams on the following pages represent the more significant changes in British merchant shipping since 1951. The variations in ships' silhouettes illustrate changes in naval architecture.

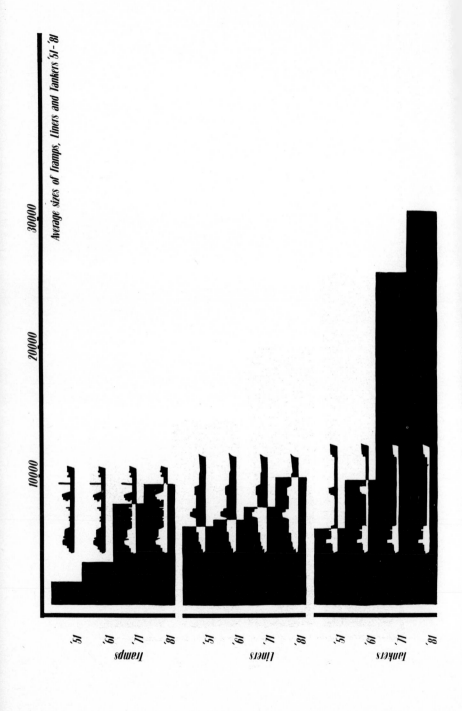

Average sizes of Tramps, Liners and Tankers '51 - '81

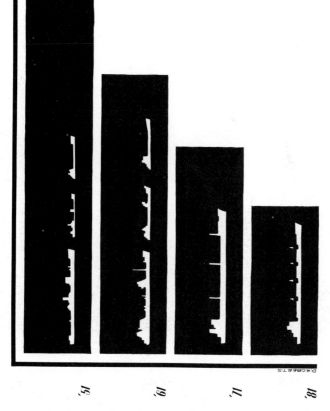

Number of Tramps '51–'81

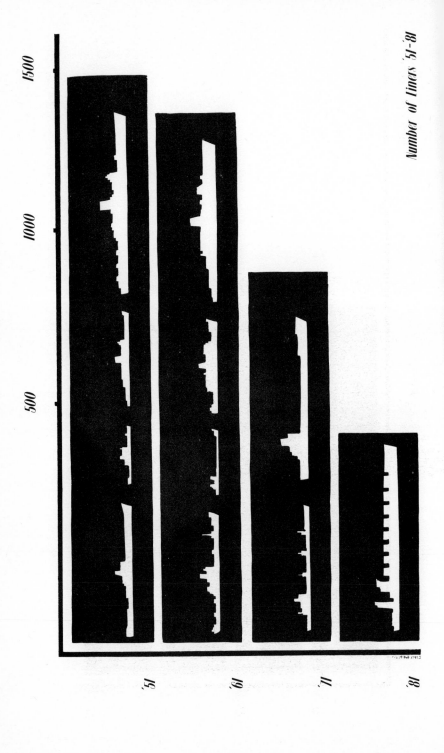

Number of liners '51-81

Number of Tankers '51 - '81

D.ROBERTS

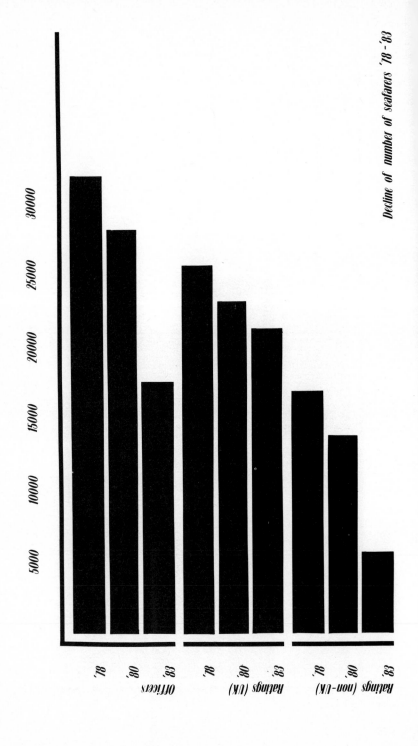

Decline of number of seafarers '78 - '83

'78	'80	'83
Officers		
'78	'80	'83
Ratings (UK)		
'78	'80	'83
Ratings (non-UK)